Black Women Filmmakers and Black Love on Screen

This book offers a thorough analysis of how romantic love between Black men and women (referred to here as Black Love) is portrayed in Hollywood films, specifically from the perspective of Black female filmmakers. Using historical and contemporary images of Black female representation in the media as a foundation, the main themes of this text focus on the male gazes' influence on Hollywood narratives, the necessity for the Black female perspective in Hollywood, and that perspective's influence on ideologies and narratives.

Brandale Mills, PhD, is a faculty member at Central New Mexico Community College in the Communications Department.

Routledge Transformations in Race and Media

Series Editors: Robin R. Means Coleman University of Michigan,
Ann Arbor
Charlton D. McIlwain New York University

Interpreting Tyler Perry
Perspectives on Race, Class, Gender, and Sexuality
Edited by Jamel Santa Cruze Bell and Ronald L. Jackson II

Black Celebrity, Racial Politics, and the Press
Framing Dissent
Sarah J. Jackson

The Cultural Politics of Colorblind TV Casting
Kristen J. Warner

The Myth of Post-Racialism in Television News
Libby Lewis

Representations of Black Women in the Media
The Damnation of Black Womanhood
Marquita Marie Gammage

Race and Contention in 21st Century U.S. Media
Edited by Jason A. Smith and Bhoomi K. Thakore

Race, Gender, and Citizenship in the African Diaspora
Travelling Blackness
Manoucheka Celeste

Media Across the African Diaspora
Content, Audiences, and Global Influence
Edited by Omotayo O. Banjo

Black Women Filmmakers and Black Love on Screen
Brandale Mills

Black Women Filmmakers
and Black Love on Screen

Brandale Mills

Routledge
Taylor & Francis Group

NEW YORK AND LONDON

First published 2019
by Routledge
52 Vanderbilt Avenue, New York, NY 10017

and by Routledge
2 Park Square, Milton Park, Abingdon, Oxon OX14 4RN

Routledge is an imprint of the Taylor & Francis Group, an informa business

© 2019 Taylor & Francis

Library of Congress Cataloging-in-Publication Data
CIP data has been applied for.

ISBN: 978-1-138-60295-3 (hbk)
ISBN: 978-0-429-46935-0 (ebk)

Typeset in Sabon
by codeMantra

Printed in the United Kingdom
by Henry Ling Limited

To the love of my life – thank you for helping me experience the true essence of Black Love.

Contents

Acknowledgments   ix

Introduction and Overview   1

1   Expressions of Black Love   17

2   The Dark Side of Black Love: Lies and Deceit   37

3   The Dependent Nurturer   45

4   Black Love and Black Feminism   58

Conclusion   73

Index   81

Acknowledgments

First and foremost, all the honor and glory goes to God, for without Him, I am nothing.

I would like to acknowledge and thank my dissertation committee for their guidance and support throughout this journey. Your support, suggestions, feedback and criticism have pushed me further than I knew I could go intellectually and academically which helped lay the foundation for this text.

Thank you to the hardest-working (finessin') cohort Howard University's CCMS Department has seen. I am forever grateful to have experienced this journey with such an amazing group of like-minded individuals. You all inspire me in different ways, and we're destined to change the world. I am also grateful to my Howard colleagues who shared their experiences and insight to help make this journey a bit easier; I will be forever grateful for your embrace and advice.

To "The Seven": you all knew me before I had dreams of changing the world. Thanks for your unwavering love, support, laughs, prayers and encouragement. You all have pushed me and motivated me continuously to be the best version of myself, and it is truly a blessing to call such an amazing group of women my besties.

To my dear friend, Allison: your tenacity is truly inspiring. You are the epitome of a superwoman and I'm so blessed to have you as a friend. My wonderful line sisters: I thank God for the gift of sisterhood. I'm so proud of each of you, and I'm glad to have you along with me on this journey.

Riley, thank you for always being my captive audience and listening ear. Cox, thank you for your unconditional love and for never letting me take myself too seriously. Although we were 1,871 miles apart while I was writing this book, your support and love surrounds me and inspires me to do wonderfully awesome things. Even if you don't really care about coding, themes and Black feminism, thank you for acting like you do.

To my mother and sister, thank you for your encouraging words and support. It is the foundation you gave me that allowed me to chase my dreams and change the world. Finally, I would like to thank all of the Black women in Hollywood both in front of the camera and behind the scenes. It is inspiring to a glimpse of my life represented through your work. Thank you for showing me and the world the diversity of a Black woman.

Introduction and Overview

Overview

I am a chronic lover of love. My movie collection is a combination of romantic and comedies and classic love stories, all of which have served as a reference point in discussions about love throughout my adulthood. In these films, there are some relationships that I despise, some that I love, some that baffle me, many that I identify with and a few that I envy which exemplify my definition of true "Black Love." Although this phrase has trended on social media and popular culture and even served as the title for a cable network television show, there has never been a tangible definition of what exactly Black Love embodies. Cultural critic and scholar bell hooks described Black Love as something that is exceptional and stemming from a place of struggle that is unique to the Black American's experience, yet Blacks are often depicted as sexual, angry and unloving in Hollywood representations (hooks, 2001).

Currently in mainstream Hollywood, romantic movies are more foolish than fun, and their content lacks sincerity and depth and the absence of Black romance in movies creates a void. Black relationships should be visible enough to be ordinary, and not always have clichéd, typical endings (Harris, 2016). The problem is not the lack of Black romances being written, but there are few Blacks in Hollywood that hold positions to green light a movie; Hollywood will only invest in Black films that White executives believe are sure moneymakers (Ivermen, 1997), despite the popularity of romance and love genres. hooks (2001) wrote, "if love is not present in our imagination, it will not be there in our lives" (p. 37); in other words, if Black audience members do not see positive images or romantic relationships in the media they consume, their lived experiences will reflect those negative depictions. She adds that gender often shapes one's perspective and this patriarchal ideology becomes particularly damaging for Black female audiences because of its impact on the systematic degradation of the African-American family structure. Black female filmmakers' limited voice could potentially shape the narratives they create, impacting the representation and identity construction of Black women.

This text offers a thorough analysis of how romantic love between Black men and women (referred to moving forward as Black Love) is portrayed in Hollywood films, specifically from the perspective of Black female filmmakers. Using historical and contemporary images of Black female representation in the media as a foundation, the main themes of this text will focus on the impact of male gazes' influence on Hollywood narratives, the necessity for the Black female perspective in Hollywood and its influence on romantic narratives.

The experience of Black women is often synonymously associated with that of Black males or White females, and very rarely recognized independently (Collins, 1990). It is this exclusion that created a space and relevancy for Black Feminist Thought's examination of the Black woman's experience, particularly in the creation of films. Using Collins' (1989) Black Feminist Thought as a theoretical framework of analysis, this manuscript also identifies feminist elements in films directed by Black women, assuming Black female filmmakers create empowering counter-narratives to negative stereotypical imagery often associated with Black women in the media. It is this notion that more diversity behind the camera contributes to more positive representations of Black women and their relationships, thus eliminating oppressive depictions of Black women. By engaging in a discussion identifying Black Feminist elements within the films under sample, the text examines the elements of the Black female experience exhibited in these films, providing implications on the Black female filmmakers' influence on Hollywood narratives.

Theatrical releases of Hollywood films were selected for this study because films are a storytelling mechanism designed to not only entertain, but also circulate ideas about culture and its people as reflected within the larger society offering a mirrored portrayal of audience member's lived experiences and provide complete narratives with imagery that suggests compelling evidence of its socialization influence (Manatu, 2003). Considering film representations are incorporated into the knowledge base of audiences and oftentimes reinforce common stereotypes about race, class and gender roles (Eschholz, Bufkin, & Long, 2002; Manatu, 2003), this text's focus on Black female directors provides insight on how marginalized groups view and depict themselves. Film directors have been described as magicians who create a lived situation through narratives and projected images, and they are ultimately responsible for the artistic and commercial success of the movie; in other words, directors manage the creative process (Morley & Silver, 1977). The director occupies a central and indispensable role and is responsible for carrying out that vision through involvement on each stage of project development (Erigha, 2018).

The creative control and freedom asserted by directors ultimately shape the narratives of movies, including how characters are portrayed and how concepts are illustrated and conceptualized on screen, thus supporting this text's emphasis on examining narratives directed by Black women. Therefore, all movies directed by Black women, including heterosexual romantic relationships, regardless of movie genre, were included in the sample with no minimum or maximum number of characters used for analyzation. Additionally, this study included films fitting these criteria from Hollywood's inception, to movies released by December 2015, as no movies released after that fit the parameters. The films under examination include: *Eve's Bayou* (1997) and *Black Nativity* (2013) directed by Kasi Lemmons, *Love & Basketball* (2000) and *Beyond the Lights* (2014) directed by Gina Prince-Bythewood, *Love Don't Cost a Thing* (2003) directed by Troy Beyer, *Cadillac Records* (2008) directed by Darnell Martin, *Something New* (2006) and *Just Wright* (2010) directed by Sanaa Hamri, *Belle* (2013) directed by Amma Asante, *Peeples* (2013) directed by Tina Gordan Chism and *Selma* (2015) directed by Ava DuVernay.

The introduction provides a historical background of Black representation in Hollywood since its inception, the history of the Black female filmmaker and Black feminism in Hollywood, and previews Black love depictions in film.

Introduction

In recent year, Hollywood has seen an increase in the number of Black women represented on the big screen, often in groundbreaking roles. The 2017 summer blockbuster film, *Girls Trip*, featuring Queen Latifah, Jada Pinkett Smith, Tiffany Haddish and Regina Hall as best friends traveling to New Orleans for the Essence Festival, illustrated the shift in how Black women are represented on the big screen; it provided a multidimensional representation, straying from historic depictions of Black women in the media. The film, which chronicled the sisterhood and trials often encountered throughout friendship, proved to Hollywood that films written by, produced by and starring African-Americans were capable of grossing over $100 million (Mendelson, 2017). While the film's success highlighted the buying power of Black audiences, there has been an increased appreciation of diverse casts creating more opportunities for Black actresses and a narrative that strayed from the stereotypical plots featuring gangs, drugs and single-parent households; Black women are still plagued with negative stereotypical images on-screen (Adams-Bass, Stevenson, & Kotzin, 2014).

Historically, Black women have been victims of negative representation because mainstream American media perpetuates stereotypes in a way that may cultivate identity and one's understanding of a group (Ashley, 2014). Some researchers have argued Black women are finally seeing progression in how they are represented on screen (Cartier, 2014), while others note traces of stereotypical imagery within pop culture's narratives (Moody, 2012). Despite the discrepancies that may exist surrounding the level of progression Black women have made, examining the narratives surrounding Black women and their contribution to persistent and pervasive Hollywood narratives is important in understanding the perpetual inclusion of offensive representations. Scholars (Adams-Bass et al., 2014; Erigha, 2015b; Mgadmi, 2009) note the negative stereotypical images of Black women have been a mainstay in Hollywood, partly because of the limited opportunities Black women have to contribute to the narratives and storylines that depict their experiences. This is particularly true with Black Love representations in the media.

The lack of women and minorities in behind-the-scenes positions in Hollywood leads to the perpetuation of stereotypical images about minorities and women (Hollywood Diversity Report, 2015). For example, Smith and Choueiti's (2011) analysis of the top grossing fictional films in 2010 found the films directed by White men were more likely to depict Black female characters as overly sexual or promiscuous. The White male-dominant ideology not only perpetuates stereotypes in film, but normalizes those beliefs within society. Even when representations of Black women are present in film, their presence is there to serve others (hooks, 2003). The problem with men, Black or White, dictating love relationship behavior to Black women is that it may perpetuate patriarchal ideals of gender roles and behaviors within romantic relationships between heterosexual Black men and heterosexual Black women. American cinema has created narratives, images and sometimes myths about American culture, with the majority of the orchestrators of those narratives being White men, while the stories from women as well as ethnic minorities often go unheard. Racial and gender inequality in the Hollywood film industry leads to the prevalence and dissemination of stereotypes, creating a problematic trend of disadvantages and missed opportunities for audience members and potential employees. Women and minorities remain underrepresented in Hollywood far below their proportion of the US population, making Hollywood a predominantly White and male sphere (Erigha, 2015a). One has to ask how the lack of diverse representation behind the scenes of Hollywood impacts and contributes to the images seen in movies.

Racial minorities were vastly underrepresented in major studios. In 2009, over 93 percent of Hollywood studio directors from the six largest film companies were White and male (Erigha, 2015a). There seemed to be no shift in 2013, where only 6.5 percent of top-grossing Hollywood films had Black directors (Smith, Choueiti, & Pieper, 2014). In movie directing, the percentage of women Hollywood directors has yet to reach 10 percent, with women's imprint on film directing declining over time (Erigha, 2015b). The Hollywood Diversity Report (2015) summarizes these statistics by stating Whites comprise two to one film directing positions compared to their minority counterparts, and three to one as film writers. Not only are minorities disproportionately represented in

Hollywood positions, but women face a greater challenge when it comes to inclusion.

With the lack of diversity among women and ethnic minorities in Hollywood, White men exercise cultural imperialism and hegemony with complete control over the images and narratives available for audiences (Erigha, 2015a). Not only do these biased images influence social behavior, but they leave marginalized audience members wondering, "What about me?" If there are no Black women behind the screen, especially in the role of a director, who will create accurate reflections of audience members in that group? Without adequate representation in media, certain groups lose the ability to create and share images and narratives that help shape the awareness of their identity and existence (Erigha, 2015a). Through adequate representation in films both as behind the scenes and as actors, underrepresented groups have the ability to counteract stereotypes, while dismantling White hegemonic ideologies.

Particularly, the Black feminist plays a unique role in the construction of narratives in Hollywood. Their stories occupy a space that many audience members desire to see in movies. The White male gaze that dominates Hollywood neglects the comprehensive reflection of Black women's experiences, and the Black woman filmmaker creates an alternative discourse informed and motivated by Black women. Black feminist films create a space where Black women do not have to resist or internalize an oppositional reading of films; instead, the viewer is more aligned with the intended message created by the filmmaker (Missouri, 2015). Through self-representation, Black women filmmakers can use cinema not only as a site of struggle, but also as a site of transformation to redefine the narratives (Ryan, 2004).

The White male-dominant ideology not only perpetuates stereotypes in film, but also tells audience members Black people are not loving, and their lives are so filled with violence and aggression that they have no time to love (hooks, 2001). Viewers exposed to a high level of romance media will come to cultivate beliefs and expectations of relationships consistent with dominant themes in the media (Johnson & Holmes, 2009). hooks (2001) said the majority of images of Blacks do not teach love. Instead, they reinforce narratives of Blackness as hateful and unloving. Examining the perspective and experiences of those creating the narratives of movies provides a better understanding of how many of these characters are developed. hooks (2000) urged audience members to consider the extent to which gender shapes a writer's perspective, specifically about love.

Hollywood's Foundation

Since its inception, Hollywood has played an instrumental role in the mass dissemination of popular culture (Erigha, 2015a). D.W. Griffith's

The Birth of a Nation (1915) was the first feature film and has been labeled as the most slanderous anti-Negro movie ever released (Bogle, 2001). The movie was a propaganda tool to reinforce the ideology that Blacks in America needed to be controlled in order to maintain social order in Reconstructed America. In the film, Griffith portrayed three varieties of Blacks, creating what would come to be known as stereotypical depictions in the early years of Hollywood: the mammy, Uncle Tom and the brutal Black bucks shamelessly provided the foundation for other films to follow for years to come (Bogle, 2001). *The Birth of a Nation* (1915) was Hollywood's reference of how to represent Black manhood and womanhood, relegating them to certain spaces such as kitchens, and in supporting roles such as criminals. This movie was the foundation of the suppression of Blackness on movie screens monopolized by White-owned and operated movie companies (Diawara, 1993). Blacks were prominent subjects in Hollywood's racist symbolic relations that continued to reproduce White-dominated racial norms (Quinn, 2012), laying the foundation for the negative stereotypical roles that Blacks in Hollywood continue to fight.

By 1918, Hollywood emerged as the film capital of the world (Bogle, 2001). During the 1920s and 1930s, independent Black filmmakers began creating realistic portrayals of Blacks, unlike their White counterparts (Bogle, 2001). This included America's first legendary Black filmmaker, Oscar Micheaux. His movies, often referred as race films, gave Blacks the opportunity to write, direct, produce and act in films more reflective of their lived experiences. Before racial integration thanks to writers like Micheaux, Black viewers experienced pleasure in viewing themselves on the screen (hooks, 2003). As Hollywood began to include more Black actors in films by the mid-1960s, race movies fought to compete, but could not match the machine known as Hollywood. Film historian Thomas Cripps said Hollywood films during this time began to reinforce hope and diverted Black attention away from the goal of an independent movie (Quinn, 2012). Many actors who had continuous roles in race films found they had no place in Hollywood. Although Hollywood has proven to be more inclusive in recent years, the ability to maximize profits has a direct impact on who is cast in films, oftentimes neglecting Black actors.

Hollywood must attract audiences and audiences seek gratification in the media products they consume (Smith-Shomade, 2002). It is this reciprocal relationship that influences the type of content created within Hollywood in an effort to generate the most revenue. Historically, Hollywood representation of African-Americans has been used as a means to connect to diverse audiences and generate more profit (Beltrán, 2005). Black narratives have become a Hollywood commodity, encouraging the creation of dozens of films that include that formula (Lott, 1991). This commodification of Black culture impacts the type of narratives displayed in the films. Hollywood continues to capitalize off the evolution of the acceptance of Black culture through the narratives, films and television shows it creates (Beltrán, 2005). These dynamics puts pressure on the director to create a movie that generates revenue, rather than creating narratives reflective of their lived experiences. In examining racial integration in the 21th century, the Hollywood film industry as a global disseminator of ideologies, and popular culture remains a barometer to measure racial inequality in the culture industries (Erigha, 2016).

The Black Female Filmmaker

Combined, Black female writers and directors barely reach 1 percent in Hollywood behind-the-camera roles. Research shows the employment of women and racial and ethnic minorities behind the scenes positively impacts the quality of on-screen images, while an absence may create less empowered characters (Erigha, 2015a). Because mainstream images of Black women are informed by stereotyped societal attitudes, challenging these narratives has become a source of struggle of many Black women filmmakers (Gibson-Hudson, 1998). It is worth examining what types of narratives these women create given the limited opportunities they have in Hollywood. These women have a small opening to counter the male-dominated portrayals that inundate audiences with stereotypes and oppressive images.

Black women filmmakers incorporate alternative, nonconventional elements of cultural history, stimulating the formation of representations in movies. Black female filmmakers present diverse images of Black womanhood that come from a realistic perspective (Gibson-Hudson, 1998). According to Gibson-Hudson (1998), these elements are important because they help recount the past and document the maturation of Black womanhood. In reclaiming narratives of Black women, it is the responsibility of the Black female filmmaker to eradicate the ideologies of dominant culture (Collins, 1986). The narrowness of the roles given to women in movies leaves little room to compete with these images that have been widely accepted by the majority audiences. There are no multifaceted roles available for Black women to counterbalance the overtly sexual images typically seen in movies (Manatu, 2003). While female directors and writers find the greatest success in the romance genre (Erigha, 2015a), it is important to note just because they are women, it does not mean they are only qualified to discuss issues of love and romance.

Black female filmmakers have the ability to create literary narratives dismantling the ideologies about Black women that are frequently seen in movies (Ryan, 2004). Hobson (2005) noted Black women who do have access to visual and literary tools of media have created new representations of Black female bodies and have resisted the objectification efforts of dominant culture. The Black female filmmakers who challenge misrepresentations of Black women seek to celebrate Blackness and womanhood (Gibson-Hudson, 1998). She added that those filmmakers create fluid and multidimensional images, adding to the relationship between representation, cultural identity and the politics of race, sex and class (Gibson-Hudson, 1998). Missouri (2015) also supported this point, quoting author Judylyn S. Ryan's statement that Black female filmmakers have the power to repossess the image of Black women and create a space where multiple female voices can be heard.

For example, producer, director and writer Carol Munday Lawrence said she makes movies to express herself and share with others and because she feels a personal responsibility to use her gifts to empower and celebrate other African-Americans (Bobo, 1998). Griffith (2001) echoed these sentiments, stating that, as a filmmaker, she plays a role in perpetuating the power of dissocializing the ideology that systematically excludes and demonizes women and people of color. It is this liberation that Black female filmmakers seek for audience members viewing their work (Griffith, 2001). A true Black feminist film serves as a tool for liberation, countering negative images of Black women (Missouri, 2015). Euzhan Palcy, the first Black woman to direct a Hollywood feature film, said it is important and urgent for women to make movies to provide a counter point of view (Donalson, 2003).

In the midst of these stark statistics in media dominated by Whites and men, directors like Ava DuVernay have achieved an unprecedented level of success for Black women (Erigha, 2015b). DuVernay was the first Black female director to receive a Golden Globe nomination. DuVernay released feature films *I Will Follow* (2010) and *Middle of Nowhere* (2012) before releasing the blockbuster hit *Selma* (2014), which chronicled a portion of Dr. Martin Luther King's life during an urgent call for voting rights (biography.com). DuVernay made film history when *Selma* (2014) received an Oscar nomination for Best Picture. She also directed Disney's *A Wrinkle in Time* (2018) movie adaptation, making her the first Black woman to direct a $100 million film, which also made her the first Black female director to have a film gross $100 million in a domestic box office (Ifeanyi, 2018; McNary, 2016; Quackenbush, 2016). DuVernay is currently directing the DC Comics movie adaptation of *New Gods*, making her the second woman to direct a superhero film (Ifeanyi, 2018). In a 2011 *New York Times* article, DuVernay said filmmakers who specifically write Black movies should understand "no one is ever going to care about their film except for the people it's made for, which is Black people" (Cieply, 2011). This statement illustrates not only the difficulty in reaching diverse audience, but also the responsibility Black filmmakers have to create content specifically for Black audiences.

Black female filmmaker Gina Prince-Bythewood, writer and director of *Love & Basketball* (2000) and *Beyond the Lights* (2014), expressed difficulty in finding marketability of Black Love in Hollywood, noting that oftentimes complex movies about Black couples are not popular among decision makers (Carter, 2014). "What I want to focus on are people of color in my films, and specifically women; they're never an easy sell" (Carter, 2014). Prince-Bythewood said she feels responsible for not only creating impactful films, but she also wants to create films that help women recognize their self-worth (Carter, 2014). It is this sense of responsibility that impacts the themes and representations present within movies.

Julie Dash's *Daughters of the Dust* (1991) is regarded as the model, both thematically and technically, for Black women's cinema. Not only was this movie an example for a wide-ranging illustration of Black women, but it was a progressive depiction of family, friendship and, perhaps most importantly, love. The film counters the erasure of Black women and their stories, erasing the invisibility of Black women in film (Guerrero, 1993). The audience's reception of this movie proves a Black woman's perspective offers an insightful and expansive view of the political vision, thus informing Black feminist filmmaking (Ryan, 2004). Dash's feminist work in both *Illusions* (1982) and *Daughters of the Dust* (1991) includes elements of her cultural background and experiences as a Black woman. In discussing how she felt Hollywood neglected her as a Black female audience member, Dash exclaimed, "I make films because I was such a spectator!" (hooks, 2003, p. 101). This outward articulation is imperative for Black female audiences to finally see images reflective of their lives without the negative impact from the consistent themes in White-dominated messaging. Dash's work as a Black feminist filmmaker supports Patricia Hill Collins' notion that ideas created by Black women reinforce the Black woman's standpoint (Collins, 1990).

Although these Black female media content creators have achieved success in a male-dominated industry, it is important to remember between 2000 and 2016, Black people directed about 7 percent of Hollywood films, with less than 1 percent of movies directed by Black women. This equates to Black women directing two Hollywood distributed films in a given year (Erigha, 2015b).

While scholars suggest diversity behind the camera is important for more culturally inclusiveness on screen representations of Black women, it is important to evaluate the connection between Black female directors and their potential impact on the shift in the dominant White narratives. Black female filmmakers are a rarity in Hollywood and their body of work, narratives and character development is worth examining to better understand how diversity behind the scenes equates to a more inclusive portrayal of Black women on screen. Black women have played such a limited role in creation of their experiences on screen that it is important to measure the impact of their contributions to creating multidimensional characters. Underrepresentation in the creation of film images limits groups from including their worldview in popular American culture (Erigha, 2018), and this is especially true as it relates to depictions of Black love.

Love Depictions in Hollywood

Love is a universal concept in human relationships depicted in art and music, and is also a recurring theme in popular media (Hetsroni, 2012). Although romance movies are often associated with concepts of love, it is important to note romance and love are different. hooks (1999) marked the distinction between romance and love, stating the media often aids in facilitating the notion that romance is a project crafted by women, and men thoughtlessly follow the lead. The fairytale version of two souls who meet, join and live happily thereafter is childhood fantasy, according to hooks (1999).

In their analysis of romantic movies, Hefner and Wilson (2013) found four themes that were prevalent in the examined films: (1) idealization of other, (2) love at first sight, (3) soul mate/one and only and (4) love conquers all. They also noted viewers who are repeatedly exposed to content like this eventually adopt the beliefs of these storylines (Hefner & Wilson, 2013). This behavior adaptation is problematic specifically as it relates to negative portrayals of romantic relationships among Black couples. If audience members are likely to adopt behaviors of romantic depictions in movies, as Hefner and Wilson (2013) concluded, Black audience members are left at a huge disadvantage because of the lack of positive imagery.

Hefner and Wilson's findings also measured physical and relational aggression in romantic relationships finding participants exposed to both physical and relational aggression in the media were more likely to be aggressive in their romantic relationships. These findings suggest dysfunctional and violent relationship depictions in the media directly impact audience members' interactions within their romantic relationship. Connecting these findings with Manatu (2003) and hooks' (1999) stance that movies rarely depict Black romantic relationships lovingly, this imagery could potentially have a severe impact on the overall state of Black relationships within our culture.

Black Love in Films

The common cliché "love has no color" may be true, but Jankowiak and Fischer (1992) noted Eurocentric views are directly linked to the appearance of romantic notions of love. For Blacks, the ambiguous definition and pursuit of love are exasperated by popular culture's overemphasis of the production and consumption of Black sex (Utley, 2010). Considering this, representations of love among Black couples in the media were very limited when compared to depictions of White couples, specifically revolving around the Eurocentric definition of love. Additionally, the ongoing argument among scholars about the inaccurate portrayals of Blacks in the media is also a concern when discussing images of Black romantic love in the media. hooks (2001) argued mass media portrays Black people as unloving and aggressive, and stated if Black audiences do not see images of positive love in the media, it will not be present in their lives. Understanding these contrasting images are important, but measuring the potential impact, influence and effect on audience members should also be an issue of concern among communication scholars.

In the early 1900s, Black Love portrayals were only acceptable when presented in a comedic fashion (McClure, 2016). The history of Black representation is so infiltrated with negative images that it can be difficult to create narratives that do not reinforce a negative racist history, especially as it fits into the dominative narratives in mass media (Wanzo, 2011). McClure (2016) described romantic narratives created by Blacks during the early 1900s as progressive, and a sharp contrast to contemporary representations of Black Love. Because of the overall marginality of Blacks in Hollywood during the 1980s, Black filmmaking's responses to Hollywood's repression of Black romance and intimacy were rare. It was during this time that Black filmmakers recognized the importance of depicting Black love and sexuality as essential in accurately depicting Black humanity (Guerrero, 1993). Veteran actress Ruby Dee, who appeared in her first movie in 1949, never starred opposite a Black man in a love story. "You've received a certain type of propaganda about yourselves, about your relationships, about White people. Something creeps in of the enemy's propaganda," Dee said in a 1997 *Washington Post* article (Ivermen, 1997). Similarly, filmmaker Spike Lee has attempted to humanize Black sexuality, but has had problems getting his film past cinemas' censorship (Guerrero, 1993).

Media representations and depictions help shape audience members' understanding and conceptualization of many concepts and ideas. Depictions of romantic love in the media could potentially have implications of audience members' perception of the world. These representations socialize our identities and how we coexist in our relationships, especially romantic relationships. More specifically, portrayals of African-Americans involved in romantic love relationships, or Black Love, are not only limited, but oftentimes inaccurate representations of the reality many audience members experience (Johnson, 2012). While love has been a consistent construct in the cultural norms of our society, images defining and representing love in the media have evolved since the inception of film. Essentially, these depictions influence audience members' interactions in romantic relationships (Johnson, 2012). Depending on the type of portrayals, this can be problematic to social interaction within the Black community.

There are a growing number of movies about romance from a Black woman's perspective. Coustaut (1998) noted the ultimate political statement for African-Americans is for audiences to see Black women and men loving each other regardless of inherent difficulties. It is this fundamental symbol of unity and togetherness that gives the Black community a representation it desperately needs (Coustaut, 1998). Unfortunately, these positive images are rarely seen, and when they are, they reduce women to sex objects. Coustaut (1998) noted all romance stories do not have to be fairytales, and they should portray realism for audiences.

Allen (2013) compared two independent films, *Love Jones* (1997) and *Medicine for Melancholy* (2008), in an effort to see how Black love movies evolved through generations. By using these movies as cultural markers to measure progression, Allen (2013) took a unique approach in comparing the narratives of the couples in the two movies. Ultimately, she found Hollywood did not change its depictions of the Black "hippie" lifestyle, and the love discourse in these movies relied heavily on clichéd tropes of Black identity (Allen, 2013). The study's findings suggested Black filmmakers may have good intentions to create liberating characters that stray from the norm, but oftentimes their stories follow the same themes of romance seen in the past.

hooks (2001) contended images in the media, specifically Black romance, directly influence audience members' understandings and behavior. Haferkamp (1999) found high television viewing was associated with the belief there were differences between the sexes, and conflict was expected between the sexes. This research supported the ideology that increased exposure to narratives in the media could potentially impact and shift audience behavior.

Manatu (2003) found portrayals of Black Love tend to marginalize and sexualize Black women (Manatu, 2003). Black women do not experience love in the media, and if they do, these images are often created by men who objectify their sexuality (hooks, 1999; Manatu, 2003). Black women are often excluded from the conversations about romance, due to a long history of being understood as hypersexual or asexual (Warner, 2015). Several scholars (hooks, 1999; Manatu, 2003; Wanzo, 2011) have highlighted the impact of gendered narratives and the need for more accurate representation. Coustaut (1998) noted even when women are depicted in romantic relationships, they are often seen as victims, simply because they are women.

Some movies are trailblazers among multidimensional depictions of Black women's lives. In Bobo's (2005) interviews of Black female viewers of *Waiting to Exhale*, she found audience members connected with the actresses, specifically because the movie focused on certain aspects of their lives, including romance. According to Bobo (2005), these depictions showed women as well-rounded, multidimensional characters who countered traditional stereotypes. These women extract images of power from these images and relate them to their everyday lives (Bobo, 1993). The emergence of Black male filmmakers has altered the images of Black female sexuality. Black women who have made valuable contributions to society have yet to see valuable reflections of themselves in movies. The media insists on presenting Black women in substandard roles of the oversexed Jezebel, the prostitute, the superwoman and the aggressive, intimidating bitch (Manatu, 2003). Simply put, Black women do not fall in love in films. They have sex; they do not make love. They do not experience love in the media, and if they do, the discourse is constructed by men (Manatu, 2003). This male gaze dominates movies and creates characters lacking a comprehensive depiction of Black women's reality. The idea of Black women's knowledge may conflict with the male-authored narratives because these authors are incapable of speaking from a Black woman's standpoint or even from a standpoint of their own that does not devalue a Black woman. Utley (2010) noted we cannot know what role love plays in our lives until we define and understand what love is, especially as it is portrayed in popular discourse. This text not only defines Black Love from the perspective of a Black woman, but also explores some of the characteristics and themes associated with the often abstract emotion.

References

Adams-Bass, V. N., Stevenson, H. C., & Kotzin, D. S. (2014). Measuring the meaning of black media stereotypes and their relationship to the racial identity, black history knowledge, and racial socialization of African American youth. *Journal of Black Studies*, 45(5), 367–395.

Allen, R. (2013). From love to melancholy: The evolution of the Black Bohemian identity in Black indie love films from Gen-X to Gen-Y. *Journal of Black Studies*, 44(5), 508–528.

Ashley, W. (2014). The angry black woman: The impact of pejorative stereotypes on psychotherapy with black women. *Social Work in Public Health*, 29(1), 27–34.

Beltrán, M. C. (2005). The new Hollywood racelessness: Only the fast, furious (and multiracial) will survive. *Cinema Journal*, 44(2), 50–67.

Bobo, J. (1993). Reading through the text: The black woman as audience. In M. Diawara (Eds.), *Black American cinema* (pp. 272–283). New York, NY: Routledge.

Bobo, J. (1998). *Black women film and video artists*. New York, NY: Routledge.

Bobo, J. (2005). *Black women as cultural readers*. New York, NY: Columbia University Press.

Bogle, D. (2001). *Toms, coons, mulattoes, mammies, and bucks: An interpretive history of Blacks in American films*. Bloomsbury Publishing.

Carter, K. (2014a, November 5). *The young black romance movie everyone said no to finally sees the light*. Retrieved from http://www.buzzfeed.com/kelley

lcarter/the-young-black-romance-movie-everyone-said-no-to-finally-se?utm_
term=.gl1Emj65B#.eyYnykxEK.

Cartier, N. (2014b). Black women on-screen as future texts: A new look at black
pop culture representations. *Cinema Journal, 53*(4), 150–157.

Ciepley, M. (2013, June 1). Coming Soon a Breakout Year for Black Films. *New
York Times.* Retrieved from http://www.nytimes.com/2013/06/02/movies/
coming-soon-a-breakout-for-black-filmmakers.html.

Collins, P. H. (1986). Learning from the outsider within: The sociological significance of black feminist thought. *Social Problems, 33*(6), S14–S32.

Collins, P. H. (1989). The social construction of black feminist thought. *Signs,
14*(4), 745–773.

Collins, P. H. (1990). *Black feminist thought: Knowledge, consciousness, and
the politics of empowerment.* New York, NY: Routledge.

Coustaut, C. (1998). Love on my mind: Creating black women's love stories. In
J. Bobo (Ed.), *Black women, film & video artists* (pp. 140–151). New York,
NY: Routledge.

Davis, A. Z., Guidry, C., Stern, J., Kitt, S., Lee, S., & Prince-Bythwood, G.
(director). (2000). *Love & basketball.*

Diawara, M. (1993). *Black American cinema.* Los Angeles, CA: Psychology
Press.

Donalson, M. (2003). *Black directors in Hollywood.* Austin, TX: University of
Texas Press.

Erigha, M. (2015a). Race, gender, Hollywood: Representation in cultural production and digital media's potential for change. *Sociology Compass, 9*(1),
78–89.

Erigha, M. (2015b). Shonda Rhimes, scandal, and the politics of crossing over.
The Black Scholar, 45(1), 10–15.

Erigha, M. (2016). Do African Americans direct science fiction or blockbuster
Franchise movies? Race, genre, and contemporary Hollywood. *Journal of
Black Studies, 47*(6), 550–569.

Erigha, M. (2018). On the margins: Black directors and the persistence of racial inequality in twenty-first century Hollywood. *Ethnic and Racial Studies,
41*(7), 1217–1234.

Eschholz, S., Bufkin, J., & Long, J. (2002). Symbolic reality bites: Women
and racial/ethnic minorities in modern film. *Sociological Spectrum, 22*(3),
299–334.

Gibson-Hudson, G. J. (1998). The ties that bind: Cinematic representations by
black women filmmakers. *Quarterly Review of Film & Video, 15*(2), 25–44.

Griffith, C. A. (2001). Below the line: (Re) calibrating the filmic gaze. In Bobo,
J. (Eds.) *Black feminist cultural criticism* (p. 85). Malden, MA: Blackwell
Publishers.

Guerrero, E. (1993). *Framing blackness: The African American image in film.*
Philadelphia, PA: Temple University Press.

Haferkamp, C. J. (1999). Beliefs about relationships in relation to television
viewing, soap opera viewing, and self-monitoring. *Current Psychology, 18*(2),
193–204.

Harris, H. (2016). *Why We Need More Black Romance Movies.* Retrieved from
http://www.indiewire.com/article/why-we-need-more-black-romance-movies-
20160224.

Hetsroni, A. (2012). Associations between television viewing and love styles: An interpretation using cultivation theory. *Psychological Reports, 110*(1), 35–50.

Hefner, V., & Wilson, B. J. (2013). From love at first sight to soul mate: The influence of romantic ideals in popular films on young people's beliefs about relationships. *Communication Monographs, 80*(2), 150–175.

Hollywood Diversity Report: http://www.bunchecenter.ucla.edu/wp-content/uploads/2015/02/2015-Hollywood-Diversity-Report-2-25-15.pdf.

Hooks, B. (2000). *All about love: New visions.* New York, NY: William Morrow.

Hooks, B. (2001). *Salvation: Black people and love.* New York, NY: William Morrow.

Hooks, B. (2003). The oppositional gaze: Black female spectators. In *The Feminism and Visual Culture Reader* (pp. 107–118).

Hobson, J. (2005). *Venus in the dark: Blackness and beauty in popular culture.* Routledge.

Ifeanyi, KC. (2018, June 6). *Ava DuVernay becomes the first black woman to direct a $100 million-grossing film.* Retrieved from https://www.fastcompany.com/40587453/ava-duvernay-becomes-the-first-black-woman-to-direct-a-100-million-grossing-film.

Ivermen, E. (1997, May 25). *What about Black Romance.* Retrieved from https://www.washingtonpost.com/archive/lifestyle/style/1997/05/25/what-about-black-romance/583228ee-30f6-428a-b614-fd1270a90e87/.

Jankowiak, W. R., & Fischer, E. F. (1992). A cross-cultural perspective on romantic love. *Ethnology, 31*(2), 149–155.

Johnson, C. (2012). *Where's the love: Portrayals of African American romantic relationships in the media.* Retrieved from http://caravel.sc.edu/2012/09/wheres-the-love-portrayals-of-african-american-romantic-relationships-in-the-media/.

Johnson, K. R., & Holmes, B. M. (2009). Contradictory messages: A content analysis of Hollywood-produced romantic comedy feature films. *Communication Quarterly, 57*(3), 352–373.

Lott, T. L. (1991, July). A no-theory theory of contemporary black cinema. *Black American Literature Forum, 25*(2), 221–236.

Manatu, N. (2003). *African American women and sexuality in the cinema.* NC: McFarland.

McClure, D. (2016). *Interface of blackface and black love: Despite the stereotypes romance prevails.* Retrieved from http://iraaa.museum.hamptonu.edu/page/Interface-of-Blackface-and-Black-Love.

McNary, D. (2016, February 23). *Ava DuVernay to direct 'A Wrinkle in Time' movie adaptation.* Retrieved from http://variety.com/2016/film/news/ava-duvernay-wrinkle-in-time-movie-1201712895/.

Mendelson, S. (2017, August 18). *Box office: 'Girls Trip' crossed $100M by being an event movie for adult Women.* Retrieved from https://www.forbes.com/sites/scottmendelson/2017/08/18/box-office-girls-trip-crossed-100m-by-being-an-event-movie-for-adult-women/#5ff807537d57.

Mgadmi, M. (2009). Black women's identity: Stereotypes, respectability and passionlessness (1890–1930). *Revue LISA/LISA e-journal. Littératures, Histoire des Idées, Images, Sociétés du Monde Anglophone–Literature, History of Ideas, Images and Societies of the English-speaking World, 7*(1), 40–55.

Missouri, M. A. (2015). *Black magic woman and narrative film*. New York, NY: Palgrave Macmillan.

Moody, M. (2012). From Jezebel to Ho: An analysis of creative and imaginative shared representations of African-American women. *Journal of Research on Women and Gender, 3*(1), 74–94.

Morley, E., & Silver, A. (1977). A film director's approach to managing creativity. *Harvard Business Review, 55*(2), 59–70.

Quackenbush, C. (2016, August 3). *Ava DuVernay is the first African-American woman to direct a $100 million film*. Retrieved from http://motto.time.com/4438223/ava-duvernay-100-million-film/.

Quinn, E. (2012). Closing doors: Hollywood, affirmative action, and the revitalization of conservative racial politics. *Journal of American History, 99*(2), 466–491.

Ryan, J. S. (2004). Outing the black feminist filmmaker in Julie Dash's Illusions. *Signs, 30*(1), 1319–1344.

Smith, S. L., Choueiti, M., & Pieper, K. (2014). Race/ethnicity in 600 popular films: Examining on screen portrayals and behind the camera diversity. *Media, diversity, & social change initiative*, 202007-2013.

Smith-Shomade, B. E. (2002). *Shaded lives: African-American women and television*. New Brunswick, NJ: Rutgers University Press.

Utley, E. A. (2010). "I Used to Love Him": Exploring the miseducation about black love and sex. *Critical Studies in Media Communication, 27*(3), 291–308.

Wanzo, R. (2011). Black love is not a fairytale. *Poroi, 7*(2), 1–18.

Warner, K. J. (2015). If loving Olitz is wrong, I don't wanna be right: ABC's Scandal and the affect of Black female desire. *The Black Scholar, 45*(1), 16–20.

1 Expressions of Black Love

Love Defined

The popularity of romance movies and films' and its ability to impact audience members may support the argument that audience members seek out these movies in order to learn more about romance (Hefner and Wilson, 2013). Because of this influence, Manatu (2003) noted films are a storytelling mechanism designed not only to entertain, but to circulate ideas about culture and its people as reflected within the larger society. Most viewers do not view media images and storylines without being impacted in some way (Eschholz, Bufkin, & Long, 2002). Media representations are incorporated into the knowledge base of audiences, and if these images are biased, they play a key role in reinforcing common stereotypes about race, class and gender roles. Although movies may be entertaining, they also provide viewers with ideas and may impact the overall perspective viewers have on marginalized groups (Eschholz et al., 2002; Manatu, 2003). Films have the ability to connect with audiences because of their portrayals of "mirrored" lived experiences of audience members (Manatu, 2003, p. 38) and often rely heavily on unrealistic portrayals of romantic and sexual relationships to appeal to their audiences (Johnson & Holmes, 2009). Most researchers believe television presents a distorted view of romantic relationships (Osborn, 2012) and if this holds true, this creates potentially damaging narratives of Black Love for audience members.

Hendrick and Hendrick (1986) developed theories about types of love, which serve as the foundation for this text's analysis of the type of romantic love seen in the movies examined.

Hendrick and Hendrick (1986) extended an existing theory of the six basic love styles in their scale development to measure each style. These styles included:

1   Eros: Strong physical preferences, early attraction and intensity of emotion attributed to erotic love, along with strong commitment to the lover.
2   Ludus: Love as an interaction game to be played out with diverse partners. Deception of the lover is acceptable.

3   Storge: Reflects an inclination to merge love and friendship.
4   Pragma: Rational calculation with a focus on desired attributes of the lover.
5   Mania: "Symptom love," based on the uncertainty of self and the lover.
6   Agape: All-giving, nondemanding love.

Sternberg's (1986) triangular theory of love encapsulates and simply defines the components of love; when combined, they illustrate the ideal experience of love. The triangular theory of love states that live can be understood in terms of three components – intimacy, passion and decision/commitment (Sternberg, 1986). While each of these terms can be combined in various ways, according to Sternberg (1986) they serve as the foundation for our basic understanding of love.

Additionally, the styles of love are often displayed through the "Five Love Languages" defined by marriage therapist Dr. Gary Chapman. Through decades of research and counseling couples, Chapman (2010) identified words of affirmation, acts of service, receiving gifts, quality time and physical touch as the primary ways all couples involved in romantic relationships give and receive love. In other words, it is through these actions that the majority of individuals in romantic relationships communicate their love to their significant other, and whether they feel loved in their romantic relationships.

"Words of affirmation" refers to individuals who verbally affirm their significant other and feel loved when they receive verbal affirmation. "Acts of service" states individuals who prefer their significant other perform tasks such as cleaning or taking out the trash are more likely to feel or experience love. If an individual's love language is "receiving gifts," they feel loved when their significant other gives them gifts. Displaying love through the "quality time" love language refers to the time spent between significant others. The "physical touch" love language points to individuals who feel loved when their significant other touches them (Chapman, 2010).

While Hendrick and Hendrick (1986) provided a basic understanding of the Eurocentric ideas of love, in her scholarship, hooks (2000, 2001, 2003) takes the concept of love, specifically connecting it to Black families in American culture. It is this contrast that provided the foundation for this text's definition of Black Love. Although hooks (2000) never explicitly labeled Black Love, one must understand how Black women define and experience love, and it is this perspective that helped shape the analysis of the movies in this sample. To fully analyze and assess portrayals of love, hooks (2000) stated definitions are the starting point of understanding.

Scholars have noted the crisis of Black people experiencing lovelessness, and hooks (2001) identified the need for research to address the issue of love among Black people and its relevance to political struggle. It is this struggle that impacted Black women's ability to create a loving home in the midst of a racist world. Most Black people's relationship to love has been shaped by trauma (hooks, 2001). Blacks have fought for the privilege of having their relationships recognized, solidifying their bond, which was also crucial to the freedom struggle (hooks, 2001). According to hooks (2001), Black Love is often about survival because of its scarcity in Black households. However dysfunctional it may be, it is this foundation that provided the foundation for the definition on Black Love. Despite this struggle, Black Love flourished when Black women and men worked together to sustain their bonds and nurture their families (hooks, 2001).

hooks (2003) described the Black female's first encounter with love shaped by patriarchal values, stating she feels as if she must earn love, that she must be good to be loved. She adds Black women often feel that in order to know love, they must be loved by others (hooks, 2003). hooks (2000) noted women are sometimes apprehensive about discussing love, out of the fear that it may appear as though they are desperate for the attention of a man. hooks (2000, 2001, 2003) noted the negative association between Black women and the topic of love, highlighting society's lack of a commonly understood meaning of love. With this understanding, the act of loving would not be so mystifying, according to hooks (2000).

hooks (2000) provided perhaps the only scholarly definition of Black Love by first describing the dictionary's definition of love, which emphasizes romantic love as "profoundly tender, passionate affection for another person, especially when based on sexual attraction" (p. 3). hooks (2000) extended this superficial definition by referring to psychiatrist M. Scott Peck's definition of love as

> the will to extend one's self for the purpose of nurturing one's own or another's spiritual growth.... Love is as love does. Love is an act of will – namely both an intention and an action. Will also implies choice. We do not have to love. We choose to love.
>
> (p. 4)

She added, in order to truly love, we must learn to mix various ingredients – care, affection, recognition, respect, commitment, trust and honest and open communication (hooks, 2000). What makes Black Love unique is that "bonds of affection and love that are forced in the midst of profound trauma and oppression have a resiliency that can inspire and sustain generations" (hooks, 2001, p. 155).

Both hooks (2000) and Hendrick and Hendrick (1986) offer different perspectives in their approach to defining love. hooks' (2000) definition countered the more widely accepted assumption that we love instinctually, while Hendrick and Hendrick's (1986) Six Basic Love Styles offer a surface, superficial examination of the concept. hooks' (2000) inclusion of multiple elements, combined with Black couples' foundation, highlights the difficulties of defining an abstract concept despite its wide usage.

Expressions of Black Love

In total, the sample consisted of 12 movies. Within the 12 films, there were 19 romantic relationships that were essential to driving the overall plots of the films, with 11 of the relationships serving as the primary or leading relationship in the movies for analysis.

Evidence of the "Six Types of Love" (Hendrick & Hendrick, 1986) was identified in the films including: passionate love, game-playing love, friendship love, practical love, possessive/dependent love and altruistic love. Hefner and Wilson's (2013) common love themes in movies – idealization of others, love at first sight, soul mate/one and only and love conquers all – in addition to bell hooks' (2009) definition of love – care, affection, recognition, respect, commitment, trust, honest and open communication and intention – were also included to assess how love was portrayed in the films. Additionally, major relationship obstacles were identified, which included infidelity, trust, lack of quality time and the woman's personal desires ignored.

Love was commonly displayed through physical affection (kissing and lovemaking), acts of service (providing for the family) and words of affirmation (saying "I love you" or other public declarations of affection or intent). Ten of the couples evaluated displayed elements of eros, or passionate love, with nine of the couples displaying agape or altruistic love, the all-giving love that, according to Hendrick and Hendrick (1986), is the type of love all individuals should seek in their relationships. Using bell hooks' (2000) definition of love, care was the most common characteristic exhibited in the character's interaction, with nearly 80 percent of the couples displaying caring elements.

There were common themes in how couples interacted with one another and how they displayed affection. All of the female characters in the sample were loyal to their significant others, meaning they did not cheat physically or emotionally. The women were also very nurturing, encouraging and supportive of their significant other. The primary means of expressing love with their partner included kissing, lovemaking or sex and words of affirmation.

Referring to Chapman's (2010) "Five Love Languages," physical affection was among the most popular displays of love, with kissing and lovemaking/sex being the primary means of expression. This supports Chapman's (2010) acts of service, considering many of the female characters were financially supported by their significant others. Additionally, words of affirmation were commonly seen as a way to express love between the couples in the sample.

Fifty-seven percent of the women in the study used physical affection as a way to express their love to their significant other. Among those, 47 percent of the sample had sex during the movie. Although Black women are often oversexualized and portrayed as sexually deviant in the media (Bobo, 2005; hooks, 2003; Missouri, 2015; Rosenthal & Lobel, 2016), this study found a contradiction to previous scholarship, considering less than half of the women in the sample were even shown having sex. For those that were, it was nonaggressive and loving. For example, the sex scene in *Love & Basketball* (2000), a coming of age story about two teenagers – Monica (Sanaa Lathan) and Quincy (Omar Epps) – and their love for basketball, was gentle and affectionate. Quincy caressed her and ensured she was comfortable during the experience, while Monica wore her mother's pearls during the experience, to imply purity and delicacy. This carefully crafted exchange counters portrayals of Black couples as unloving and sexually aggressive.

Fifty percent of the male characters in the sample were the primary breadwinners in their relationships, with many of their significant others feeling loved because they were financially provided for. This was the case for Louis Batiste (Samuel L. Jackson) in *Eve's Bayou* (1997), film about a young girl, Eve Batiste (Jurnee Smollett), and her discovery of her father's extramarital affairs that take an unfortunate toll on his entire family. In one scene, Eve asked her mother Roz (Lynn Whitfield) about her dad's long work hours, her mother responded, "Listen, you little ingrate. Your father works hard so we can have a house with four bathrooms!" Although Roz knew her husband was cheating, she excused his behavior because of what he provided for her and their children.

Nathan Wright, Monica's father in *Love & Basketball* (2000), was the primary breadwinner for his family in the film. Camille, Monica's mother, was frequently seen performing traditional household duties such as cleaning, cooking and ironing, while her husband who was often depicted in work clothes was portrayed as the head of the household. In the same film, Zeke McCall, ex-NBA player, was the breadwinner for his wife Nona and son Quincy. Nona, however, was not a doting wife, satisfied by what her husband provided. Although Zeke was the primary breadwinner of the family, it also came with a cost. His philandering and late nights because of work began to wear on Nona and their relationship (this dynamic will be discussed in later chapters).

Muddy Waters was also the primary breadwinner in his relationship with Geneva Wade in the film *Cadillac Records* (2008), the musical drama that documented the true-life story of the Chicago record label that introduced legendary artists as Howlin' Wolf, Little Walter, Etta James and Chuck Berry. Although Geneva was a nurse and was often shown in her professional attire, Muddy showered her with lavish gifts and even purchased her a home. Similarly, *Selma* (2015), a film that chronicled the historic civil rights marches led by Dr. Martin Luther King, Jr., depicted Martin as the sole breadwinner for his wife Coretta and their children. Despite supporting his family's livelihood, Coretta was happy with many elements of their relationship, one being his lack of quality time spent with his family. These relationships will be discussed in greater details in later chapters.

Elements of words of affirmation were also seen in the movies, although not as prevalent as acts of service and physical affection. Many of the main male characters said they loved their significant others and cared about them immensely, despite their contradictory unfaithful behavior (discussed in later chapters). For example, *Talk to Me*'s (2007) Petey Greene (Don Cheadle) often used his humor to compliment his girlfriend, Vernell Watson (Taraji P. Henson), in the film depicting the Washington, DC radio personality Ralph Waldo "Petey" Green. He would tell her she's "fine as frog's hair" or "baby, I tell you how good you look?" Despite their arguing, their interaction was playful and expressive. Her support for Petey was apparent, as she was always encouraging him.

Belle's (2013) John Davinier had no problem verbally expressing his love for Belle, despite the potential backlash he was subjected to. "I love her! I love her with every breath I breathe!" he told her uncle, who was opposed to their romantic relationship. John later told Belle, "I cannot conceive a life without you. I love you for all that you are and all that I am."

Quality time, or lack thereof, was also a major point of contention between many of the couples in the sample. The majority of the couples analyzed displayed quality time as a way to express love to their significant other. Gina Prince-Bythewood's movies, *Love & Basketball* (2000) and *Beyond the Lights* (2014), displayed the most amount of quality time between the main couples. During their college courtship, Monica and Quincy were portrayed as inseparable. They walked to class together, supported each other at their basketball games and spent time with each other in their dorms. Prince-Bythewood used the amount of quality time to show the intimacy of Monica and Quincy's relationship. There was an apparent sense of connectivity between the two that solidified the bond associated with their relationship.

As NBA basketball star, Scott McKnight's (Common), physical therapist Leslie Wright (Queen Latifah), the two spent a considerable amount of time together in *Something New* (2010), a film about Scott's rehabilitation after a devastating injury with Leslie's assistance. When Leslie moves into Scott's home full-time to help him recover, they share many special moments where each becomes vulnerable with one another. In a montage sequence, Hamri shows the couple running together, eating together, laughing together and sharing intimate moments. It is this display of quality time that solidifies their relationship and establishes them as more than just friends. Without this quality time that was spent between them, they ultimately would not have fallen in love and progressed their relationship.

There were also elements of words of affirmation in the film when during an interview about his career comeback, he credited his success to Leslie's rehabilitation. He said:

> She saw something in me that I didn't even see in myself. She believed in me so much, she practically willed me back to the game. It was a lot of hard work and even when I was in pain and wanted to quit, she wouldn't let me. Instead she made me laugh. Instead, Leslie, she made me laugh. Somehow, she made the worst three months of my life the best three months of my life. I wouldn't be here without her.

This outward display of affection and declaration truly embody Chapman's (2010) definition of words of affirmation.

The 2006 romance, *Something New,* a film about a professionally successful woman, Kenya McQueen (Sanaa Lathan), and her journey to find love in an unconventional relationship, also displayed elements of quality time. Kenya's relationship with her landscaper, Brian Kelly (Simon Baker), is particularly notable in this examination because of Brian's race – he's White. Through Kenya's struggle to accept Brian's race and their cultural differences as it related to their relationship, they spent a considerable amount of time together getting to know each other. The couple was seen shopping together, dining together and attending social events with one another. The quality time spent between Kenya and Brian helped fortify their relationship and was the ultimate reason why Kenya fell for him.

Similarly, in *Beyond the Lights* (2014), a film about a romance between a young singer reaching stardom and a young cop with political ambitions, Noni Jean (Gugu Mbatha-Raw) and Kaz Nicol (Nate Parker) spent a great deal of quality time with each other during the early phases of their relationship, providing a visual of how the closeness between them was achieved. The more time they spent together, the greater amount of self-disclosure was shared between them, increasing their connection. Their intimacy was visible, which allowed them to grow as a couple, aiding in Noni's self-discovery. Noni incorporated Kaz into her world as an entertainer, with him serving as her personal bodyguard throughout her busy schedule. And at the climax of the film, Prince-Bythewood used the couple's trip to a secluded area of Mexico as a turning point for their relationship, solidifying their bond and connection.

The couples who displayed quality time as a way to express and receive love often were resistant to spending time with their suitors, but because of the time shared together, they eventually grew closer.

This commonality was no different for the film, *Love Don't Cost a Thing* (2003), starring Nick Cannon as Alvin, a nerdy teenager who convinced popular cheerleader, Paris (Christina Milian), to be his girlfriend for two weeks after agreeing to do the repairs on her parents' truck for free. Although the couple began as an odd pair, their chemistry developed as they spent more quality time together at school, shopping and attending parties together. Similar to Noni in *Beyond the Lights* (2014), Paris allowed herself to be vulnerable with Alvin, disclosing intimate details of her life. This intimacy would not have been achieved without the quality time spent together.

On the contrary, 65 percent of the remaining couples made specific and implicit mentions of the lack of presence of their significant other. For example, there was evident tension and resentment between Coretta Scott King and Martin Luther King, Jr. in *Selma* (2015), which viewers can assume was a result of Martin's busy travel schedule. There were scenes when Martin reluctantly told Coretta about his travel plans, because he understood the toll his absence had on his role as a father and husband. Based on the five love languages, the audience only saw acts of service displayed between Coretta and Martin, despite the obvious reverence between them. Coretta came to Selma unexpectedly to support Martin during this difficult feat, after recently confronting Martin about his infidelities. For them, this support served as an illustrator of love.

While many of the men used Chapman's (2010) love languages to express their love to their partner, their infidelity contradicted their actions. This leads one to conflicting messages about how love is defined. Can one truly love their significant other when they are not being honest with them and cheating on them? I will discuss how love is defined in later sections.

Six Love Styles

Hendrick and Hendrick's (1986) "Six Love Styles" include passionate love, game-playing love, friendship love, practical love, possessive/dependent love and altruistic love. As seen in Table 1.1, the two most common love styles displayed in this sample were eros, or passionate love, and agape, or altruistic love.

Although many of the couples in the sample displayed moments of intense passion with each other, they did not mirror depictions of oversexualization, as other scholars (Manatu, 2003; Missouri, 2015) have noted. The filmmakers used the passion to illustrate the intense attraction between the couples, rather than their connection being purely based on sex. Even in situations where eros was the only love style displayed, the researcher did not feel like there was a lack of love between the characters in these moments of passion. For example, there were several scenes throughout *Talk to Me* (2007) where Petey and Vernell were overly physically affectionate.

Table 1.1 Six Love Types in Films

	Eros	Ludus	Storge	Pragma	Mania	Agape
Eve's Bayou	X	X	X	X	X	X
Love & Basketball	X	X	X	X	X	X
Love Don't Cost a Thing	X	X	X	X		X
Something New	X			X		X
Talk to Me	X					X
Cadillac Records	X			X	X	X
Just Wright	X		X			X
Belle			X	X		X
Beyond the Lights	X					X
Black Nativity				X		X
Peeples		X				X
Selma				X		X

These results seem a bit contradictory, considering many of these re-lationships dealt with issues of infidelity. Yet, the female characters in these relationships still managed to love their partner unselfishly. With half of the sample's study encompassing altruistic love, the reciprocal, unconditional love was evident in the relationship depictions, despite the tribulations these relationships may have endured. Perhaps the forgive-ness and acceptance of their partner's infidelities provides a new defini-tion for unconditional love.

Characteristics of Black Love

While scholar, author and feminist bell hooks (2000) did not provide an explicit definition of "Black Love," she used care, affection, recogni-tion, respect, commitment, trust, honest and open communication and intention as characteristics that embody the essence of love. In apply-ing her concepts to the depictions of love in movies directed by Black women, there were some commonalities in how these Black directors understand, comprehend and describe love, supporting Black Feminist Thought's notion that Black women's experiences are a heterogeneous collective notion (Collins, 2000).

As Table 1.2 illustrates, over half of Hollywood films directed by Black women exhibited all of the characteristics of love defined by hooks. Con-tradicting the historical definition of the Tragic Mulatto, both Noni Jean and Belle, although categorized as Tragic Mulatto in this sample, experi-enced love comprised of all the elements outlined by hooks. Additionally,

Table 1.2 bell hooks' (2009) Definition of Love in Films

	Care	Affection	Recognition	Respect	Commitment	Trust	Honest and Open Communication	Intention
Eve's Bayou	X	X	X	X	X	X	X	X
Love & Basketball	X	X	X	X	X	X	X	X
Love Don't Cost a Thing	X	X	X	X	X		X	
Something New	X	X	X	X	X	X	X	X
Talk to Me	X	X	X		X			
Cadillac Records	X	X	X		X			X
Just Wright	X	X	X	X	X		X	X
Belle	X	X	X	X	X	X	X	X
Black Nativity	X	X		X	X	X	X	X
Peeples	X	X			X	X	X	X
Selma	X		X	X	X	X	X	X

Mozelle Batiste Delacroix, Eve's aunt in *Eve's Bayou* (1997), experienced this all-encompassing love with her significant other, Julian.

In *Beyond the Lights* (2014), Noni and Kaz's relationship went through various stages, but by the end of the movie, all elements of hooks' characteristics of love were evident. Early in their relationship, Kaz was the protector and provider for Noni. Not only did he save her life on the balcony after her suicide attempt, but he often went above and beyond to protect her and her reputation. He defended his relationship with Noni to his father and was both literally and figuratively a nurse to Noni's wounds. Kaz provided a safe space for Noni to be transparent. During a conversation where Noni described her inability to reveal her true self to those in the industry, she said, "No one cares what I have to say." Kaz responded lovingly, "I'm listening." While everyone in Noni's entourage was trying to profit off her celebrity, Kaz took the opposite approach; he was genuinely interested in knowing the Noni behind the public image.

Similarly, Belle and her love interest John Davinier displayed elements of a comprehensive love as described by hooks. Despite society's rejection of Belle because of her Black heritage, John embraced that, telling her any man should be willing to accept and love her completely. Unlike her other suitor, Oliver, who considered her mixed race a flaw he was willing to overlook. "I pray he would marry you without a penny to your name, for that is a man who truly treasures you," John said to her.

Belle's pessimism about love was apparent early in the movie. Belle told her cousin who was constantly gushing about potential love pursuits, "You shouldn't love because it will leave you poor and brokenhearted," also telling her that "love must be a very complicated thing." With this thinking as her foundation, it was no surprise when she accepted the marriage proposal from Oliver, her self-centered suitor. When her cousin jealously asked her how it felt to be engaged, Belle responded, with little emotion, "Perfect." Asante used Belle's relationship with Oliver and John to provide a juxtaposition illustrating true, unconditional love, versus the superficial relationship displayed between her and Oliver. In this contrast, the union between John and Belle was positively depicted because his love allowed her to embrace her identity. He not only accepted her Blackness, but he encouraged her to embrace it.

As the movie progressed and Belle evaluated her romantic interests, she was plagued with a conflicting decision to make the practical choice and marry Oliver to increase her social status, or follow her heart and marry John, whose courtship would bring her no financial or social status benefit. Her relationship with John provided a sense of release for her to finally embrace the unconditional love she had been fighting for her entire life. In a climactic moment in the movie, John professed his love for Belle to her great-uncle, saying, "I love her! I love her with every breath I breathe!" Although she did not immediately reciprocate those feelings verbally, she eventually told him, "I cannot conceive a life without you... I love you for all that you are and all that I am."

Belle achieved her happily ever after in a relationship that seemed to encompass all the positive characteristics hooks (1999) described. This outward act of love was a feat for the Black woman's depiction of love, because it countered common ideologies stating Black women (especially biracial women) are often portrayed in the media as unloving, unlovable and incapable of being in functional, loving relationships (hooks, 1999).

Although Mozelle, the town's clairvoyant, was not a leading protagonist in *Eve's Bayou* (1997), her relationships provided an interesting juxtaposition to the other depictions in the film. Mozelle's characteristics are often attributed to men, due to her self-disclosed infidelities and multiple long-term relationships. Mozelle thought she was "cursed" because all her husbands died while married to her. In a pivotal scene, Mozelle described the love she experienced with her previous husbands after Eve asked her which one she loved the best. She replied, "I don't know, Eve. They was all different. Anderson was the handsomest man I've ever seen. Your uncle Harry, he was the sweetest. And Maynard ... Maynard loved me most of all." Each of her relationships was critical in shaping her identity.

Despite being labeled a "black widow" when Mozelle met Julian, the epitome of an all-encompassing love relationship, he disregarded her attempts to keep him away, providing her with each element of hooks' definition of love. He told her, "You're wounded here (placing his hand on her heart), and it's here that I'll plant seeds." It is through this relationship Mozelle reached her fullest potential in a romantic relationship. She was visibly at peace with Julian, further supporting hooks' definition of love as universal.

Kenya was initially resistant to her all-encompassing love in *Something New* (2006) with Brian, largely because he was White. She had a preconceived notion of characteristics of her perfect mate, or her "ideal Black man," and Brian did not fit into that prototype. She was uptight career woman, who hated animals and lacked spontaneity with dreams of marrying a "fine Black man," while Brian was a landscaping engineer who loved working outside with his dog. The two were an unlikely pair, but as their relationship evolved, it displayed all elements of hooks' characteristics of love. Race, however, played an intricate role in the progression of their relationship. For example, Kenya ended their first date abruptly after Brian asked her if she dated White men. She said, "I just happen to prefer Black men. It's not a prejudice, it's a preference." They eventually began dating, but it was clear Kenya was uncomfortable with dating a White man, avoiding inviting him to family events. In an intimate scene between the couple, Brian told Kenya, "I know you're sensitive about color so we'll take it slow. No one has to know if we don't want them to. We'll let this be our little secret." They were clearly from two different worlds, but after an argument about race, Brian attempted to show Kenya he was committed to their relationship.

I want to be there for you, Kenya and we can talk about whatever you like. I may not be able to connect, but I promise I'll empathize, because it would be a shame to let something so superficial get in our way. It's challenging, but aren't we up for the challenge? Kenya, I love you.

Regardless of how much Kenya resisted letting Brian in her life, he embodied all of the characteristics of her ideal mate and when she finally accepted him, she allowed herself to be love and be loved unconditionally.

As previously mentioned, Scott's public declaration of love for Leslie during an interview in *Something New* (2006), not only were they words of affirmation, but they also illustrated Scott's care, affection, recognition, respect, commitment, trust, honest and open communication and intention. Their relationship came full circle as each of those elements was displayed and reciprocated by both Leslie and Scott as their connection flourished, but it was not realized until that moment.

Black Love Conquers All

This "love conquers all" philosophy was adopted from the four themes Hefner and Wilson (2013) found as prevalent in 52 highest grossing romantic comedies since the early 2000s. These themes included: (1) idealization of others, (2) love at first sight, (3) soul mate/one and only and (4) love conquers all to examine additional themes in romantic movies. While there were elements of idealization of others, love at first sight and soul mate/one and only, "love conquers all" was the most prevalent theme of Hollywood films directed by Black women, with 42 percent of the couples exhibiting these characteristics. Sixty-six percent of the films in this sample exhibited elements of love conquers all, which is consistent with Hefner and Wilson's (2013) findings. Also similar to Hefner and Wilson's (2013) findings, the couples in the sample did not have perfect relationships absent from trials and obstacles, but they overcame these difficulties in order to reach their idealistic relationship. Oftentimes, these idealistic relationships did not empower women or give them a sense of agency within their relationships.

Perhaps the best example of love conquers all in the movies examined was the relationship between *Love & Basketball*'s (2000) protagonists, Quincy and Monica. Six years after their breakup due to Quincy's infidelities, Monica professed her love saying, "I've loved you since I was 11 and the shit won't go away." Despite the tribulations their relationship endured, she still loved him as purely and innocently as when they were children. After that statement, they agreed to play a basketball game, wagering the future of their relationship. If Monica won, Quincy would call off his engagement; if Quincy won, Monica agreed to buy him a wedding gift. Initially, Quincy won the game, telling Monica, "All is fair in love and basketball, right?" But he quickly disregarded the terms of the bet, telling her, "Double or nothing."

The couple seemed to disregard the circumstances that led to the demise of their relationship six years prior, solely relying on their love to sustain the longevity of their relationship. Neither of them addressed the ramifications of Quincy ending his engagement a week before the wedding, or the potential obstacles they may encounter as a couple who have not spoken to one another in years. In *Love & Basketball* (2000) love was a game to be won and their happy ending supports the notion that despite issues that may have impacted or hindered the overall success of a relationship, love countered that, in turn conquering all.

Another example of "love conquering all" was seen in Troy Beyer's movie, *Love Don't Cost a Thing*. As previously mentioned, high school nerd, Alvin Johnson, repaired the car of popular cheerleader, Paris Morgan, in exchange for her pretending to be his girlfriend for two weeks, but before Alvin's transformation to popularity, he admired Paris' beauty from afar often gazing at her while she walked down the hallway, displaying elements of idealization of others. Throughout the duration of their relationship, Alvin gained popularity and self-confidence, which eventually pushed Paris away. Alvin was no longer dependent on Paris to help craft his image; instead he became cocky, disregarding Paris and her efforts. Upset, Paris eventually exposed Alvin and their bet in front of the entire senior class, embarrassing Alvin in the process. The pivotal moment in the movie came when Alvin embraced his true identity and decided not to try to fit in with the popular crowd, prompting Paris to profess her love for him. They forgave one another and ended the film with a passionate kiss.

Despite embarrassing each other with hurtful words and actions, Paris and Alvin pursued a relationship that was essentially founded on a lie. Their strong feelings, or love, were enough to make them overlook the difficult things they experienced. Although they experienced challenges, similar to Hefner and Wilson's findings (2013), these challenges were presented as a means for them to overcome and reach that idealistic stage of love.

Beyond the Lights' (2014) protagonists Noni and Kaz also overcame difficult obstacles in their relationship to display love conquers all elements. The couple experienced dishonesty, identity issues and lack of support of their relationship from their friends and family, yet their love for each other was strong enough to keep them connected. Much of the depiction illustrated an "us against the world" theme, as they often found solace with each other secluded from the outside world.

As Noni went through her transition from the public persona that was created for her, to embracing her true self, she shared with Kaz her desires for her professional life and their relationship. It was during this evolution that Kaz began to believe the "real" Noni had emerged. Unfortunately, Noni disappointed him as she reverted to embracing her old ways. The couple broke up, and in a reconciliation attempt, Noni embraced the idealistic relationship, telling Kaz, "It (their relationship) was perfect ... what we had..." He responded, "We started on a lie, so it could never be perfect." Neither considered or even addressed the idea that it was impossible to have a perfect relationship. Instead, it seemed like the norm to strive for perfection, however unrealistic that may have been. After Noni recognized her faults in the relationship and in other areas of her life, Kaz appreciated these changes, surprising her at a European concert and telling her, "I love you and I'm not taking it back this time." Again, love conquers all.

As previously mentioned, *Just Wright*'s (2010) characters Leslie Wright and Scott McKnight's relationship evolved after Leslie helped Scott rehabilitate is potentially career ending injury. But before Leslie fell in love with Scott, her approach to love embodied the love-conquers-all mentality. In the beginning of the film, Leslie said, "I haven't found the one I'm looking for. The one I can't live without." Shortly later in the film, Leslie asks her father, "When am I going to meet that one amazing guy who feels like I'm the one he can't live without?" While these are common trends in films and reality, it encompasses Hefner and Wilson's (2013) theme that there is a singular soul mate, or only one person who you are supposed to marry and live happily ever after with. Leslie ideology supports the notion that there is some sort of a predetermined destiny for those looking for love.

Leslie and Scott's relationship hit a critical point, when Scott's exgirlfriend, Morgan, showed up to his house proclaiming her love for him. Ironically, her visit happened the morning after Scott and Leslie consummated their relationship, forcing Scott to decide who he wanted to continue dating. Scott chose to go back to Morgan, leaving Leslie devastated and prompting her to search for a career out of state. It was during Scott's interview, detailed earlier in the chapter, that he realized he wanted to be with Leslie and he was determined to win back her love. He traveled to Philadelphia, where Leslie was interviewing for a position, to profess his love for her:

SCOTT: Leslie, I want to talk to you.
LESLIE: What are you doing here?
SCOTT: Look, I know you didn't want to see me, but I need...

LESLIE: You're right, I don't. Why are you here?

SCOTT: ... I'm in love with you. I know that now.

LESLIE: No, what you know now is that the woman that you were gonna marry is not the woman you thought she was. So now here you are, looking for Plan B. You want your best friend, your cheerleader, that was there for you when the chips were down? Well, guess what, Scott, I don't want to be Plan B. And I won't be that, even for Scott McKnight.

SCOTT: Listen to me, Leslie, listen. You're not my fallback plan. I'm not here 'cause things didn't work out with Morgan. Be stubborn all you want, but I know you.

LESLIE: You don't know me.

SCOTT: I know you love me. I know those feelings didn't conveniently fade away 'cause you're mad at me. And you have every right to be. But I'm not leaving these grounds without you. I'm not waking up another morning without being able to look at you next to me. Leslie, you're just right for me. And if I have to move to Philadelphia or to Cleveland or wherever I got to go, I am.

In that moment, Leslie made a call, accepting an offer with Scott's team as a physical therapist. Despite Scott abandoning Leslie for another relationship, love conquered all and the couple moved past his previous indiscretions.

Peeples (2013), a film about Wade Walker and his visit to Peeples' annual family reunion in the Hamptons to ask for his girlfriend, Grace's, hand in marriage also displayed elements of the love conquers all notion. Wade was extremely committed to his relationship with Grace, despite the fact that she hid her relationship from her family for over a year. During his visit with her family, Wade constantly tried to prove himself to her father, oftentimes creating more problems for himself. After getting kicked out of the family home, Wade traveled back to New York City alone and defeated, without Grace or permission to marry her. Back in the Hamptons, Grace reflected on her decision and ultimately chose to fight for her love with Wade. She surprised Wade at one of his performances saying, "I love you, Wade and I think you're crazy enough to love me for who I actually am." Despite the initial disapproval from her father, Grace chose love over status.

Although many of the films exhibited elements of love conquers all, *Something New* (2006), however, countered Hefner and Wilson's (2013) themes, rejecting many of the themes of idealization of others, love at first sight, soul mate one and only and love conquers all in the main protagonist's relationships. As previously described, Kenya's initial response to her relationship with Brian was less than ideal. When she met him, she was not captivated or enamored by his good looks or personality, debunking the idealization of others and love at first sight notion. Even after she began dating and falling in love for Brian, Kenya was not convinced that Brian was her soul mate, thus countering the soul mate/one and only and love conquers all notion. In fact, Kenya and Brian's relationship completely challenged the common characteristics often seen in romantic comedies (Hefner & Wilson, 2013).

Ironically, although Kenya's relationship with Brian did not display elements of Hefner and Wilson's (2013) themes, her personal ideologies were more aligned with the soul mate/one and only theme. For example, early in the film, Kenya told her friends that she has keep believing that she will find "the one." Midway through the film, Kenya met Mark Harper (Blair Underwood) a successful lawyer, who met her "ideal Black man" criteria. Although they appeared to have many things in common and shared similar professional experiences, Kenya eventually rejected Mark saying, "You're a great guy. Perfect, but this just isn't right for me." Despite dating her idealized mate, Kenya chose to pursue her unpredictable relationship with Brian saying she wanted to experience magic, a sentiment often attributed to one's soul mate.

Although Kenya and Brian's relationship did not begin as with a fairy tale beginning, they overcame their differences, highlighting a bit of the love conquers all concept. After experiencing an epiphany and deciding to go back to Brian, Kenya told him:

> I've never had to be anyone but myself with you right from the beginning, and with you, I feel like I can do anything, say anything, try anything. That's the life I want. I want an adventure with you.... We're supposed to be together. I know this is right. You're the one I want, Brian. I love you.

Brian responded saying he never stopped loving her and they eventually get married. Although their relationship took an around-about journey to embody the love-conquers-all notion, Kenya and Brian were able to overcome their racial differences that greatly impacted their relationship and allowed love to be the determining factor of their relationship's fate. Perhaps this relationship displayed the most realistic qualities often experienced in real life. For example, many people do not have the luxury to admire their love interest from afar, romanticizing aspects about their relationship. And although some people may be initially attracted to a potential love interest, the love at first sight notion is often shaped by other attributes or characteristics.

Comparing the Various Types of Love

While some elements of Hendrick and Hendrick's (1986) love styles share some similarities with hooks' characteristics of love, there are some differences noted between the two definitions. For example, Hendrick and

Hendrick's (1986) love styles identified all aspects of the way people love, addressing both the idealistic and practical ways people love. hooks' definition, however, focused primary on the positive elements that should be displayed in a loving relationship. Perhaps, the combination of these love styles and characteristics of love provides a holistic understanding of love and its functions.

This sample exhibited more elements of hooks' characteristics of love. Although only 6 of the 19 relationships encompassed all of hooks' characteristics, more than half of the relationships displayed at least two of those elements. Comparatively, most of the relationships displayed elements of the Six Love Styles embodied superficial elements that were not reflective of a comprehensive, unconditional understanding of love. This illustrates how the relationships in this sample, although surface at times, displayed a more in-depth and comprehensive portrayal of love in romantic relationships. These findings show Black filmmakers portrayed love in ways that was more inclusive and more positive than previous scholarship suggests (Coustaut, 1998; hooks, 2000; Manatu, 2003).

This text defines Black Love as accepting one's imperfections and indiscretions, employing care, affection, recognition, commitment, respect, trust, intention and honest communication for the overall progression of the relationship. This definition, however, is a bit contradictory, considering many of the relationship depictions portray elements of the ideology of White patriarchy's role in relationships. It is the acceptance and adaptation of European standards of living that blurs the lines between a working definition of Black Love. Although love cannot be defined or constrained to one's race or ethnic background, Jankowiak and Fischer (1992) noted Eurocentric views shape the definition of love, and that definition may not be applicable to Black relationships.

Although this study showed all-encompassing love is not a frequent occurrence in movies directed by Black women, the slight advancement in relationship representation provided counter-narratives to the lack of love Black women give and receive in media depictions. This study provided an additional perspective and definition of Black Love as it is seen in the media. Ultimately, these findings show the majority of the relationships in this sample have adopted the Eurocentric ideology of how romantic relationships function (Alameen-Shavers, 2016; Missouri, 2015) as previously discussed, thus impacting their expectations from their significant other's roles in the relationship.

Additionally, the romanticized themes often seen in romantic comedies as defined by Hefner and Wilson (2013) were also prevalent throughout the films examined. The point provides an interesting contradiction to the notion that Black love differs from Eurocentric examples of love.

Perhaps manufactured love in the media exhibits similar characteristics regardless of the racial background of those involved. These shared features provide an interesting examination to Black love and its connection to more widely accepted definitions of love. While scholars and popular culture suggest Black love embodies something that is purely unique to Blacks, the identified themes in these films may suggest otherwise. The following chapter will discuss additional themes and trends found within the relationships under sample.

References

Alameen-Shavers, A. (2016). The "Down ass bitch" in the reality television show *Love and Hip Hop*. In D. Allison (Ed.), *Black women's portrayals on reality television* (pp. 191–211). Lanham, MD: Lexington Books.

Bobo, J. (2005). *Black women as cultural readers*. New York, NY: Columbia University Press.

Chapman, G. (2010). *The 5 love languages of teenagers: The secret to loving teens effectively*. Chicago, IL: Moody Publishers.

Collins, P. H. (2000). Gender, black feminism, and black political economy. *The Annals of the American Academy of Political and Social Science, 568*(1), 41–53.

Coustaut, C. (1998). Love on my mind: Creating black women's love stories. In J. Bobo (Ed.), *Black women, film & video artists* (pp. 140–151). New York, NY: Routledge.

Eschholz, S., Bufkin, J., & Long, J. (2002). Symbolic reality bites: Women and racial/ethnic minorities in modern film. *Sociological Spectrum, 22*(3), 299–334.

Hefner, V., & Wilson, B. J. (2013). From love at first sight to soul mate: The influence of romantic ideals in popular films on young people's beliefs about relationships. *Communication Monographs, 80*(2), 150–175.

Hendrick, C., & Hendrick, S. (1986). A theory and method of love. *Journal of Personality and Social Psychology, 50*(2), 392.

hooks, B. (2000). *All about love: New visions*. New York, NY: William Morrow.

hooks, B. (2001). *Salvation: Black people and love*. New York, NY: William Morrow.

hooks, B. (2003). The oppositional gaze: Black female spectators. In A. Jones (Ed). *The Feminism and Visual Culture Reader* (pp. 107–118). New York, NY: Routledge.

Jankowiak, W. R., & Fischer, E. F. (1992). A cross-cultural perspective on romantic love. *Ethnology, 31*(2), 149–155.

Johnson, K. R., & Holmes, B. M. (2009). Contradictory messages: A content analysis of Hollywood-produced romantic comedy feature films. *Communication Quarterly, 57*(3), 352–373.

Manatu, N. (2003). *African American women and sexuality in the cinema*. Jefferson, NC: McFarland & Company, Inc. Publishers.

Missouri, M. A. (2015). *Black magic woman and narrative film*. New York, NY: Palgrave Macmillan.

Osborn, J. L. (2012). When TV and marriage meet: A social exchange analysis of the impact of television viewing on marital satisfaction and commitment. *Mass Communication and Society, 15*(5), 739–757.

Rosenthal, L., & Lobel, M. (2016). Stereotypes of black American women related to sexuality and motherhood. *Psychology of Women Quarterly, 40*(3), 319–336.

Sternberg, R. J. (1986). A triangular theory of love. *Psychological review, 93*(2), 119–135.

2 The Dark Side of Black Love
Lies and Deceit

Black Love in films directed by Black women has been expressed in a variety of ways, with physical affection and acts of service as the primary way couples displayed their love for one another. More couples embodied bell hooks' all-encompassing definition of love, while many couples exhibited the belief that love overcomes all obstacles, thus impacting their ability to defeat many challenges that otherwise may be detrimental to couples. Although many of the couples employed the belief that love conquers all, oftentimes the trials that needed to be conquered were issues of infidelity and lack of quality time spent together. Two overarching themes were identified after examining these couples, including women being portrayed as the complacent nurturer and unfaithfulness creating a disconnect within the relationship. Within two of those themes, subthemes were identified (Table 2.1).

Unfaithfulness Creates a Disconnect

The most common obstacle faced by the majority of the couples examined in the study was infidelity, which was often a result of the lack of quality time spent in the relationship. While there were occurrences of infidelity without issues of quality time described as a contributing factor, there was a connection between the two in 42 percent of the couples under examination.

Table 2.1 Recurring Themes and Subthemes

Unfaithfulness Creates a Disconnect	*Dependent Nurturer*
Infidelity	Love conquers all
Lack of quality time	Financial support equates complacency

Infidelity

Half of the films included elements of infidelity, with many of the major couples in these movies addressing issues directly related to the men cheating, including the primary relationship between Quincy and Monica in *Love & Basketball* (2000). Quincy and Monica's relationship stemmed from a childhood friendship, and for a period of time in the movie, they displayed a supportive and loving relationship. Their happy relationship shifted after Quincy learned about his father's extramarital affairs, which eventually put a strain on his relationship with Monica. After confiding in Monica about his disappointment in his father's actions, he wanted her to comfort him, but that came with a cost. In order for Monica to remain a starting player on University of Southern California's (USC) basketball team the following day, she had to leave to make the team's curfew. Quincy took her unavailability personally, and the next day, he displayed his discontent by blatantly flirting with a girl in Monica's presence. Adding to Monica's humiliation, Quincy took the same woman on a date while Monica was visiting his dorm room. Later that evening, when Quincy attempted to discuss his feelings with Monica, she said, "How do I know the next time you're feeling neglected, you're not going to run around on me? If we're going to be together, I have to be able to trust you." Quincy responded, "I'm not asking for us to be together." Ultimately, his insecurities and infidelities led to the demise of their relationship during that stage of their life.

Don Cheadle's portrayal of Washington, DC, disc jockey Petey Greene in *Talk to Me* (2007), directed by Kasi Lemmons, also showed issues of infidelity throughout his relationship with his outspoken girlfriend, Vernell. Throughout the movie, Vernell proved herself to be a supporting, loyal companion, despite Petey's indiscretions. There were several sequences in the film showing Petey with other women, then getting caught by Vernell, only for her to accept him back after a brief period of separation. Their interactions at times were extremely passionate, but also very volatile. One of the most notable scenes from this interaction came when Vernell walked in on Petey having sex with a woman, and broke a beer bottle to use as a weapon. Holding the broken bottle to Petey's neck, Vernell said, "You tell this bitch how I was the only one to take your sorry ass in" (referring to allowing Greene to stay with her after he was released from prison). Vernell was a witty, fast-talking woman with plenty of street knowledge, and she also displayed loving and supportive characteristics, accepting Petey despite his flaws and infidelities.

Consistent with the theme of infidelity was Jeffrey Wright's depiction of Muddy Waters in Darnell Martin's *Cadillac Records* (2008). Muddy met his significant other, Geneva Wade (Gabrielle Union), early in the film, and they quickly began a romantic relationship while he struggled to launch his career as a musician. Almost immediately, Muddy became acclimated to the musician lifestyle, which included indulging in alcohol and women. Martin used a montage of scenes to show Muddy with several different women, buying them gifts, having sex with them.

One pivotal scene in the movie illustrating Muddy's infidelities and Wade's reluctant acceptance of his indiscretions came when Muddy came home drunk one night to find Geneva, visibly upset, sitting on their bed holding an infant girl. She said, "A woman came by today. She said she's yours. She said she couldn't take care of her anymore." In his drunken stupor, Muddy started kissing the baby and attempted to kiss Geneva. Meanwhile, Martin inserted images of him dancing and kissing other women, flashing back to Geneva in tears. Her anger and hurt were noticeable, but after quick contemplation she said, "She's going to need milk." Almost as if, in that moment, she weighed the pros and cons and decided to accept the situation. Even after Geneva learned about the child Muddy fathered outside of their relationship, he continued to have outside affairs, oftentimes bringing his other women to work engagements. Not only did this scene illustrate Muddy's continuous infidelities, but Geneva's characteristics and acceptance of his action were consistent with the definition of the dependent nurturer.

Samuel L. Jackson's portrayal of Louis Batiste in Kasi Lemmons' *Eve's Bayou* (1997) had the most tragic consequences of his infidelities compared to other men in the sample; his extramarital affair ultimately led to his death by the hands of his mistress's husband. Louis, a physician, was depicted as a hero in a small town in Louisiana. Women openly flirted with him; his mother likened their admiration for him as though they considered him the "Second Coming." His mistress, Matty Mereaux, was seen during the opening scenes of the movie dancing with Louis during a party at Batiste's house. While nobody in the moment suspected an improper relationship between the two, the following scenes introduced what ended up being a critical element of the movie. Eve, Louis's middle child, left the party and fell asleep in the carriage house, to be awakened by Louis and Matty having sex. Although the two were startled when Eve made her presence known, they quickly brushed it off, causing Eve to second-guess what she witnessed as she recalled the story to her older sister later that night.

Shortly after, Roz, Louis's wife, was shown crying on the couch, based on what is to be assumed as her acknowledgment of her husband's philandering behavior. The scene shifted to Eve eavesdropping on her mother's conversation with her aunt and grandmother (Louis's mother), and her mother said, "And I said, 'I have three of his damn babies,' how dare she call here!" Louis came home shortly after, interrupting the conversation between the three women, and made light of the situation and jokingly closed the door. This scene is particularly interesting, because it depicted Roz's support system subconsciously condoning Louis's behavior. They chastised his actions behind his back, yet they never encouraged Roz to present any consequences, which ultimately created a system of acceptance for his behavior. As Missouri (2015) noted, Roz maintained her role as a dutiful wife, all while maintaining the façade of respectability in an attempt to maintain the White elite standards of conduct. Perhaps it was the preoccupation with maintaining a public image of high standing that impacted the director's decision to depict accepting infidelity as the norm.

Carmen Ejogo's depiction of Coretta Scott King was no exception to this system of acceptance; director Ava DuVernay brought Martin Luther King's extramarital affairs to the big screen in her 2014 movie, *Selma*. In an effort to weaken Martin's leadership, FBI Director J. Edgar Hoover used the "tension in the (King) household" to dismantle King's platform. Hoover mailed audio recordings of Martin having sex with other women to the King household. Initially Martin denied being on the tape, but Coretta confronted her husband, saying:

> I've gotten used to a lot. All of the hours wondering after your safety, worried about how you are. This house. Renting here. No foundation. Living without the things children should have all because of how it would look. I have gotten used to it. For better, for worse. But what I've never gotten used to is the death; the constant closeness to death. It's like a thick fog to me. I can't see life sometimes because of the fog of death constantly hanging over. People actually say that they will stop the blood running through the hearts of our children. That's what they said on the other end of that phone line. How they're going to kill my children. And what they'll do to you and how they'll do it. How many years have I had to listen to this? The filth, deranged and twisted and just ignorant enough to be serious.

Coretta continued, "If I ask you something, will you answer me with the truth?" King responded, "Yes." Coretta said, "Good, because I am not a fool. Do you love me?" He responded, "Yes, I love you, Coretta." She asked, "Do you love any of the others?" After a long pause, Martin responded, "No." Coretta did not discuss Martin's infidelity at any other point in the movie.

This scene was impactful, because before addressing Martin's infidelity, Coretta described everything she and their children had sacrificed to support Martin's dream. In doing that, she highlighted Martin's selfishness and disregard. Part of this sacrifice included Martin's time spent away from his children and wife. It seemed as if she understood the agency she had in this relationship and illustrated that through her description of the betrayal she felt. Coretta ironically exhibited strength in her silence.

Besides the commonality of these characters cheating on their significant other, it is important to note all of the women in these relationships stayed with their partners after learning of their affairs. This theme, which is also consistent with the dependent-nurturer definition, supports Utley's (2011) findings stating women often stay in relationships where they have experienced infidelity because they are being provided for, and the "good" in the relationships outweigh the bad. While the women in Utley's (2011) study and the characters in the movies examined felt betrayed by the indiscretions of their significant others, they stayed in their relationships. Although the female characters in the films did not explicitly state stayed in their relationships because their livelihood would be affected (because they were primarily supported by their significant others), it is assumed that fact impacted their decision to stay in the relationship. Black cultural values dictate Black women should remain faithful to their partners, supporting them at all costs (Harris & Hill, 1998) and this notion is clearly exhibited throughout these films.

As Missouri (2015) noted in her analysis of *Eve's Bayou* (1997), that movie (in addition to the others in this sample) emulated the 1960s White, middle-class family life in which "the husband/father is the all-knowing provider and the mother, regardless of education or ability, stays in the home and is expected to perform the role of submissive wife/mother" (p. 100). Alameen-Shavers (2016) extended this notion stating White patriarchy and White womanhood continues to adopt this ideology. White women do not have their own thoughts; instead they embody the same thinking of their husbands. It is this construction of patriarchy that, according to Missouri (2015), Black families mimic in an attempt to duplicate White high society.

This patriarchal model situates the father as the hero, while the woman is limited to household work, tending to the children and serving her husband (Missouri, 2015). These findings show that, despite direction from a woman, regardless of color, patriarchal ideology is still latent and evident in many of the narratives that are created. Perhaps, it is based on the experiences of these filmmakers, or perhaps these filmmakers are sticking to the narratives commonly accepted in Hollywood. Contesting these commonly processed images could create a backlash among audience members.

Forty-four percent of the movies in the sample exhibited embodiment of the White middle-class family life described by Missouri (2015). For example, Angela Bassett's portrayal of Aretha Cobbs in *Black Nativity* (2013) was laden with examples of her playing the role of a submissive wife. Despite her husband's decision that led to the strained relationship between them and their daughter, Naima (Jennifer Hudson), Aretha continued to support her husband, serving as the first lady of the church and pillar of the community. She never condemned the reverend's actions, nor held him accountable.

Lack of Quality Time

These relationships also revealed lack of quality time spent between couples with a clear connection between the lack of quality time and infidelity. Forty-two percent of the couples mentioned quality time, or lack thereof, as an obstacle in their relationships. These movies revealed that not spending time was either a result of their infidelities or helped facilitate their infidelities. Many of the male characters in the sample credited their busy work schedule as contributing factors for the lack of quality time between them and their partner, regardless of their ability to find time to maintain relationships with other women.

In addition to infidelity, Roz and Louis also encountered elements of the subtheme of lack of quality time. It was assumed Louis was frequently gone from the house during odd hours and weekends because of his career, but Roz reached a point in the film where she was fed up with the lack of time he was spending at home. As he left the dinner table to go tend to the welfare of a patient, Roz questioned him, saying, "Louis, it's Sunday." He responded, "Well, when you find a way to put sickness on an eight-hour, five-day schedule, you let me know." Roz responded angrily, "Well, what's wrong with them, they can't wait a day?" As Louis put his jacket on and walked toward the door, Roz said condescendingly, "Which one of your patients are you going to see today?" Louis responded, "Woman, go get your palm read and let me go do my work." This scene not only illustrated Roz's growing intolerance of Louis's time away from home, but also showed Louis asserting his power as the primary breadwinner of the household. Roz clearly knew Louis's time spent away from home was not strictly work related, but as this scene noted, as the sole financial supporter of the family, Roz felt like she had little room to voice her concerns.

Quincy's parents in *Love & Basketball* (2000), Nona and Zeke McCall, displayed not only issues of infidelity but also lack of quality time. After coming home late one night, Nona confronted Zeke, a former NBA player, about his job keeping him out late at night. Zeke responded, "I'm not going to get anywhere by punching a clock just so my wife doesn't get an attitude." Nona responded, "I came second to the NBA. I'm not about to come second to no bullshit scouting job." She continued, "Zeke, all I'm saying is it would be nice if you spent some time with your family." It is later revealed that Zeke was involved in extramarital affairs, one of which produced a child.

Zeke and Nona's relationship was an example of the connection between infidelity and lack of quality time. While one action may not cause the other, that conversation illustrated the potential association between the two dynamics. Forty-two percent of the characters suspected their husbands of cheating because of the lack of time they spent at home, and all characters were correct in their assumptions.

Although it is clear the media profits off the many narratives normalizing Black infidelity (Utley, 2011), Whisman and Snider (2007) stated the infidelity rates in the Black community are more prevalent than others, finding Black men are nearly twice as likely to cheat on their significant others compared to White men (Whisman & Snider, 2007). These findings support the themes found in this study, perhaps even reflecting the experiences of the Black women directing these movies. In other words, if the Black women who create these narratives experienced infidelities in their romantic relationships, those lived experiences contribute to the body of knowledge used to form discourse about love.

The major obstacles in romantic relationships identified in these movies were mainly issues of infidelity, also supporting Galician's (2004) notion that audiences view romantic content to see relationships that appear to work despite all obstacles. Considering this study found many obstacles, such as infidelity, in more than half of the relationships examined, Galician's (2004) stance perhaps explains why audiences have not rejected movies laden with dysfunction. This also explains why filmmakers create narratives with such complex obstacles. If directors know audience members enjoy viewing relationships that overcome high levels of obstacles, they may be more prone to give the audience what they want. Overcoming these obstacles contributes to the love-conquers-all notion, which as previously discussed has been noted as a prominent theme in films featuring romantic relationships. Perhaps the inclusion of these obstacles is the winning formula to attract audiences, in turn, generating more revenue for films.

But why are so few examples of Black Love directed by Black women examples of happy, functional relationships? Why are Black couples always relegated to negative representations? While research (Utley, 2011; Whisman & Snider, 2007) may support that these depictions are reality for many Black American families, one must consider whether these images impact and shape our lived experiences, or whether these portrayals serve as a mirror for Black families. Or perhaps these fictional relationships embody the unconditional, unwavering acceptance and forgiveness of one's indiscretions. While this may be true, it seems problematic for Black viewers that these relationship flaws always seem to be matters of infidelity.

References

Alameen-Shavers, A. (2016). The "Down ass bitch" in the reality television show *Love and Hip Hop*. In D. Allison (Ed.), *Black women's portrayals on reality television* (pp. 191–211). Lanham, MD: Lexington Books.

Galician, M. L. (2004). *Sex, love, and romance in the mass media: Analysis and criticism of unrealistic portrayals and their influence*. New York, NY: Routledge.

Harris, T. M., & Hill, P. S. (1998). "Waiting to Exhale" or "Breath(ing) Again": A search for identity, empowerment, and love in the 1990's. *Women and Language, 21*, 9–20.

Missouri, M. A. (2015). *Black magic woman and narrative film*. New York, NY: Palgrave Macmillan.

Utley, E. A. (2011). When better becomes worse: Black wives describe their experiences with infidelity. *Black Women, Gender & Families*, 5(1), 68–89.

Whisman, M. A., & Snyder, D. K. (2007). Sexual infidelity in a national survey of American women: Differences in prevalence and correlates as a function of method of assessment. *Journal of Family Psychology*, 21(2), 147–154.

3   The Dependent Nurturer

Stereotypical Representations of Black Women

Mainstream cultural forms are full of representations of Black women as victims, pawns or systemic oppressive forces, lacking the will or agency to resist (Bobo, 1998). If historically Black women have been portrayed as helpless or even deviant, then how do these themes impact depictions in mainstream media? Understanding stereotypical representations of Black women in the media is important in considering how these images may influence romantic depictions in Hollywood.

Criticisms of media often discuss how women and minorities are systematically limited to minor roles or roles that are consistent with traditional stereotypes (Eschholz, Bufkink, & Long, 2002). Women are clearly underrepresented throughout media, and when they are portrayed, it is in a negative manner (Collins, 2000). This is especially true for depictions of women of color. Preconceptions about women of color are perpetuated through mainstream media and serve as a focal point for popular culture. These objectifications have become mandatory images within our culture (Smith-Shomade, 2002) and shape the public's perception of African-American women and their role within society. Manatu (2003) stated audiences are rarely directed to take Black female characters seriously. Perhaps the lack of seriousness from audience members stems from the lack of character development given to Black female characters in movies. Research (Collins, 2000; Eschholz et al., 2002; Manatu, 2003; Smith-Shomade, 2002) has also described how systematic dissemination of stereotypical roles impacts audience members' perceptions of and interactions with Black women.

Research (Eschholz et al., 2002) has shown that the media typically uses stereotypes disparaging females and minorities, perpetuating those stereotypical myths. Stereotypes impact people's judgments and behaviors toward others (Rosenthal & Lobel, 2016). These portrayals imply these members occupy no significant social space (Eschholz et al., 2002). By evaluating how certain depictions in the media have evolved over time, we can identify the issues, themes and messages that audience members tend to subscribe to. Gibson-Hudson (1998) noted that Black women's images reflect patriarchal visions, myths and stereotypes and fantasies of Black womanhood. It is these representations that limit the probability of audience members viewing Black women as empowered beings.

Media consumers inundated with unrealistic portrayals of females and minorities are likelier to adopt those cultural standards based on race and sex (Eschholz et al., 2002). Similarly, Reynolds-Dobbs, Thomas and Harrison (2008) supported this notion in their research, finding mediated information influences people's perceptions of stereotyped groups, particularly when they have limited or no direct contact with the group. Not only do these findings illustrate how impactful stereotypes are when shaping a construction of understanding, but they also highlight how writers and directors in Hollywood with limited exposure to diverse groups may perpetuate stereotypes through their narratives.

Other research has focused on how to deconstruct the negative stereotypes associated with Blacks in the media (Margolis, 1999). Through her examination of Black filmmakers such as Robert Townsend and Mario Van Peebles, Margolis (1999) stated Black filmmakers hold the responsibility to contribute to how Blacks are perceived by Blacks and Whites. This responsibility, Margolis (1999) noted, should replace the negative images often associated with Blacks in the media. Bobo (2005) also illustrated this point in her research interviewing Black women on their attitudes about the movies *Waiting to Exhale, Daughters of the Dust* and *The Color Purple*. She found viewers of a movie written by a Black woman (*Daughters of the Dust*) mentioned feeling liberated and empowered by the on-screen depictions, while they noted traditional stereotypical depictions in the other two movies under analysis. Both Margolis (1999) and Bobo's (2005) research highlighted how counter-narratives are essential in illustrating the Black experience. Without the character identification from audience members, Missouri (2015) noted that Black female viewers are forced to create an alternative meaning of movies from their position of a Black woman.

In her book, *Shaded Lives: African-American Women and Television*, Smith-Shomade (2002) analyzed African-American women's positioning in the media as objects. They limited their agency and subjected them to the oppressive narratives consistent with the dominant ideologies that created them. While scholars Gamson et al. (1992) claimed the media allows for competing structures of reality, stereotypes from the Jim Crow era permeate media depictions of Black women, and these stereotypes are often embedded in narrative themes that convey the messages of racial integration and Black social mobility (Kretsedemas, 2010). The media serves as an influential source of information, which creates a convenient way of constructing stereotypes and impacts how Black women are evaluated by others and influence how people interact with them (Reynolds-Dobbs et al., 2008). For Black women, stereotypes have been used to dehumanize women, denying them of true woman-hood (Chen et al., 2012).

Film critic and author, Donald Bogle, suggested only a few roles exist for Black women in the media – the mammy, jezebel and tragic mulatto (Smith-Shomade, 2002). The mammy is distinguished by her sex and fierce independence, and she is usually big and cantankerous (Bogle, 2001). A contemporary version of the mammy is the matriarch who emasculates, controls and berates her male counterpart (Tyree, 2011).

The Jezebel is considered an alluring seductress with a limitless sex appetite (Brock, Kvasny, & Hales, 2010). This hypersexualized image conceptualizes Black women as sexually deviant and aggressive, embodying the belief that Black women have an unquenchable sexual appetite (Glenn & Cunningham, 2009). The Jezebel stereotype is important for this text's context because of its implications on how female characters may be portrayed in romantic relationships. The Jezebel stereotype is the most overtly sexual image associated with Black women; she is depicted as loose and unable to control her sexual desires (Davis & Brown, 2013). According to Brown et al. (2013), this stereotype is evident in today's media, specifically music videos, television and movies.

The Tragic Mulatto character is biracial (Black and White), and is usually portrayed as likeable (Bogle, 2001). Her on-screen experiences lead audiences to believe that she could have a normal life, if she were not plagued or victimized by divided racial inheritance and cultural ambiguity (Bogle, 2001; Missouri, 2015). She is usually portrayed as a sexually attractive, light-skinned woman of African-American heritage who could pass for White (Kretsedemas, 2010); she possesses the socially accepted desirability of the White woman (Missouri, 2015) and is struggling to "find" her place in the world (Bogle, 2001).

Reynolds-Dobbs et al. (2008) added two additional stereotypes to Bogle's roles: they define the Crazy Black Bitch as an angry, vindictive, unstable woman who is overly aggressive and untrustworthy. She is often depicted as lazy, unprofessional and argumentative, and has difficulty maintaining relationships (Reynolds-Dobbs et al., 2008). Another emerging image of Black professional women is the overachiever, known as the Superwoman (Reynolds-Dobbs et al., 2008). The Superwoman can handle large amounts of work and is intelligent, articulate, professional, strong, assertive and talented (Reynolds-Dobbs et al., 2008). These representations become concrete characters, rather than multidimensional people with actual lives, and they have little separation between the representation and the actual persons (Bobo, 2005).

Additional contemporary stereotypes of Black women in the media include the Diva, who is considered beautiful, independent and able to choose a mate based on the ability to provide upward mobility for herself (Tyree & Jones, 2015). The Black Queen is seen as a "good" mother held in high regard in the Black community. She embodies sexual purity, motherhood and spirituality (Tyree, 2009). The Baby Mama is the mother of a man's child whose relationship has ended (Tyree & Jones, 2015). The Welfare Mother is considered lazy and collects government assistance while living in poverty (Tyree, 2011). The Gold Digger is depicted as uneducated and possesses little social status, and sex is her primary commodity (Tyree, 2011). While Black women's existing stereotypes may vary in their characteristics, one commonality among several of their traits is the overarching theme of sexualization.

Sexualization of Black Women in Hollywood

Films have failed to provide audience members with images of Black women in diverse roles, providing social scripts that show people appropriate gender ideology as well as how to behave toward one another (Collins, 2004). Images of the "good girl" and the "bad girl" are reinforced as a cultural mainstay, and these depictions of Black women as sex objects have a specific function in the dissemination of stereotypes (Manatu, 2003). Collins (2004) defined sexual politics as a set of ideas and social practices that are shaped by gender, race and sexuality, that shape how men and women treat one another, as well as how men and women are treated by others. It is no surprise viewers come to accept the images that devalue Black women because of these portrayals' prevalence in movies.

The Black female body has been fetishized and identified with heightened sexuality and deviance. It has also been widely excluded from dominant culture's idea of beauty and femininity (Hobson, 2005). Because of this, Hobson (2005) stated beauty is a site for political resistance, where Black women constantly strive to redefine their bodies by reasserting their womanhood. The construction of female beauty is reflective of the racial hierarchies of White supremacy and Black subjugation, thus highlighting how certain discourses perpetuate ideologies that oppress certain groups (Hobson, 2005).

The oversexualized images of Black women stem from the 19th-century image of the African woman, Hottentot Venus. The "Hottentot" was Sarah Bartmann, an enslaved African, who was objectified and placed on public display for exhibition because her genitalia and buttocks were considered extraordinary (Davis & Brown, 2013). The introduction of Hottentot Venus represents the beginning of hypersexual images of Black women, with current representations of this same hypersexualized, animalistic image of African and Black women in Western media (Foster, 2009; Hobson, 2005). In addition to the exploitation of her sexuality, the image of Hottentot Venus was primitive and animalistic (Foster, 2009). It was this representation that rendered Black female sexuality as too deviant and too bizarre to take seriously (Hobson, 2005). These oversexualized images help shape stereotypes of Black women in the media, shaping the perception of Black women's sexuality (Davis & Brown, 2013).

Although oppressive practices such as the exploitation of Hottentot Venus have been eradicated, the continued commodification of Black sex without love cements Blacks as hypersexual deviants (Utley, 2011). Since early films, Black women have been presented as sexually deviant and dominant (Bobo, 1998). Manatu (2003) noted a dichotomous characterization between Black women and White women and their sexuality. "A paradoxical effect of the split... is the implied sexual freedom women of the dominant group can more easily express without public condemnation compared to Black women" (Manatu, 2003, p. 19). This stance supported Cartier's (2014) findings stating Black women are not portrayed as women on screen; instead they are objects subject to the narratives of dominant culture.

Although Black actresses currently have limited roles that do not objectify their sexuality, sexualized images of female celebrities historically have opened the doors for many Black actresses looking to become more mainstream (Bogle, 2007). Stars like Eartha Kitt, Joyce Bryant and Dorothy Dandridge dramatized sex, which served as their gateway to Hollywood (Bogle, 2007). During a time when Black women were overly concerned about their image, actresses such as Pam Grier saw the "sexy-vulgar-slut image" as a source of liberation (Bogle, 2007, p. 194). While these instances illustrate how Black women have used their sexual images to advance their careers, some argue these images continue to oppress women, despite the opportunities they are afforded because of them (Bogle, 2007).

Hobson (2005) noted our male-dominated culture continuously judges Black women by their physical attractiveness and compares them to standards of beauty defined by White supremacy. African-American women have been subjected to sexualized stereotypes that attack their gender and racial identities. These images often subject them to sexual exploitation and victimization as a means of dehumanizing (Brown et al., 2013). Black women are shown as sex objects, passive victims and "other" in relation to both Black and White males and White females (Gibson-Hudson, 1998). Black women also find their bodies subject to misinterpretation and mislabeling by the dominant culture (Hobson, 2005).

Foster (2009) stated controlling images of Black women shape how their sexuality is depicted. Faluyi (2015) supported this in her study of objectification of women in hip-hop culture, noting Black women's sexuality is used as a tool to be exploited for profit. Faluyi (2015) found Black female rappers do not challenge objectified representations. In fact, the study participants discounted overly sexualized behavior as a form of empowerment. In other words, Black female audience members viewing overly sexual images of Black women did not find these images liberating; instead, they felt controlled by racial stereotypes.

Manatu (2003) devoted her study to examining Black women's sexual depictions in American cinema. Manatu (2003) examined movies with Black female characters who had well-developed roles, comparing how Black male filmmakers' visions of Black women's sexuality paralleled with how White male filmmakers depicted Black women in their movies. Although she predicted racially based differences would exist in the sexual sensibilities and visions between these men, her study found no sharp difference in how Black male filmmakers portrayed Black women sexually compared to White male filmmakers. In fact, Manatu (2003) noted the Black male filmmakers portrayed these women as more sexual and promiscuous compared to their White male filmmaker counterparts.

Currently, racism has shaped Black popular culture and mass media related, contesting and reformulating Black sexuality (Collins, 2004). Manatu's (2003) study highlighted the importance of not only diversity behind the scenes of Hollywood in race, but also gender. These findings supported hooks' (1992) claim that male ideologies perpetuate stereotypical gender roles in their writing and depict Black women as overly sexual, which is consistent with historical stereotypes of Black women in the media. Manatu (2003) and hooks (1992) highlighted the void in Hollywood that Black female writers and directors could fill with their narratives and accurate representation. Diverse representations are needed behind the scenes in order to have more diverse, liberating characterizations of Black women on screen. This text found contradictions to pervasive stereotypes of Black women in the media, but also uncovered an entirely new stereotype of Black women in loving relationships – the Dependent Nurturer, a woman who is motherly and tends to the needs of the household, but is also content in her husband's infidelities, because he financially provides for her and their children.

An element of the Dependent Nurturer is the ideology that despite obstacles, infidelity or relationship struggles, the love shared between the individuals is enough to help them overcome any difficulties. Oftentimes, the women's loyalty was a direct result of the secondary role they played in their relationship, which also contributed to their complacency or dependency within their relationships. These women were nurturing homemakers who were often revered by members of their community. The women in these caregiving roles often sacrificed their personal desires, resulting in one of the common obstacles found between the couples.

The Dependent Nurturer can be defined as a woman who upholds her duties as a loving, motherly and nurturing caretaker, despite her husband's unfaithfulness. She accepts cheating from her significant other as the norm, if he provides financially for their family. As seen in half of the characters in the sample, the Dependent Nurturer loved her children and husband unconditionally, was often held in high regard within the community, worked tirelessly as a caregiver and sacrificed her personal desires (whether it be professionally or romantically) to maintain the order of her household. Even if the Dependent Nurturer did have a professional presence outside of the home, her family was her main priority and no other responsibilities superseded their importance.

Black Women Are Motherly and Complacent

Keeping in line with the characteristics of the dependent nurturer, 64 percent of the couples display and receive love through acts of service. It was implied that the women who continued in relationships knowing their significant other was unfaithful did so partly because the men were the primary breadwinners in the household. In other words, because these men provided a standard of living for their families, the male characters considered this as a way to prove their love for their significant others, despite their shortcomings. A more in-depth examination of behavior between partners and their displays of love was discussed in Chapter 1.

Acts of service, or providing for the livelihood of their significant other, was the primary way 50 percent of the men in the sample conveyed love in their relationships. Additionally, maintaining the home for their family was the primary way their female counterparts conveyed their love. In these relationships, these women were rarely shown outside of the home, and they were frequently seen doing domestic roles in the house. These findings support Utley's (2011) research stating women feel loved and taken care of when their husbands provide for them and their families, thus proving this aspect of the study's findings to be an accurate depiction of the lived experiences of many Black women.

While none of the male characters explicitly stated they were the sole providers of their household, there were several indicators in the movies that implied that notion. For example, as previously discussed, female characters such as Aretha Cobbs in *Black Nativity* (2013), Camille Wright in *Love & Basketball* (2000), Roz Batiste in *Eve's Bayou* (1997), Coretta Scott King in *Selma* (2014) and Geneva Wade in *Cadillac Records* (2008) were always seen completing domestic tasks, and never shown in a work environment. In contrast, their significant others' characterizations often revolved around their occupations. Although none of the male characters in the sample directly state providing for their families is a symbol of love, it was implied through the heavy emphasis of their devotion to their career in order to provide for their families. The roles of mother and nurturer have been intrinsic in Black culture with Black women providing the emotional support, childcare, discipline, food preparation and household maintenance for children (Harris & Hill, 1998) all exhibited in these films.

Only 30 percent of the characters in the sample exhibited characteristics consistent with the traditional stereotypes previously discussed, such as the Jezebel, Tragic Mulatto and the Crazy Black Bitch. Instead, these characters created an entirely new stereotype: the dependent nurturer.

These findings also reject the notion that Black women are not motherly or nurturing (Collins, 2004). The characters examined were often homemakers who were respected and loved by their children and other family members.

Collins (2004) contended, Black women have historically fought for roles in the media depicting them as womanly and nurturing, compared to White women, who often only get portrayed in this manner. Supporting this point, Manatu (2003) stated Black women are rarely given the opportunity to be portrayed as feminine and loving, but are often shown as aggressive and angry. This study, however, illustrated a slight irregularity from this ideal; almost half of the women in this sample were depicted as womanly, nurturing homemakers consistent with Tyree's (2009) definition of the Black Queen, a woman considered a good mother who is held in high regard in the Black community and embodies sexual purity, motherhood and spirituality.

For example, *Black Nativity*'s (2013) Aretha Cobbs' husband, who was a reverend in Harlem, told the congregation during his Christmas sermon, "I get my help from my beautiful wife. My lovely wife who has protected me and guided me through many troubles. She takes care of me in so many ways. I am blessed." This public declaration of the role she played in his life illustrates a direct contradiction to previous research stating Black women are portrayed as unlovable (hooks, 2000), bossy (Douglas, 2010) or aggressive bitches (Manatu, 2003).

Similarly, *Eve's Bayou*'s (1997) female protagonist, Roz Batiste, was highlighted as a nurturing caretaker. She took care of her three children, and was often shown cooking dinner in the kitchen, wearing aprons and tending to the children's needs. She did not appear to have a traditional job outside of as a housewife, nor did she display any affiliations outside of her husband and children. Roz was visibly the primary caretaker of her children due to her husband's busy schedule as the community doctor. Roz is among the 57 percent of female characters in the sample who enjoyed her role as a mother and wife and considered herself privileged to live such an esteemed lifestyle. She told her daughter, Cecily, "If you're lucky one day, you'll be fortunate to have a husband and children of your own," as if being a wife and mother was a coveted experience and should be considered a blessing.

Similarly, Coretta Scott King was rarely seen in *Selma* (2015) not doing any domestic work. The opening scene of the movie showed Coretta helping her husband get dressed while he prepared for an upcoming speech. Despite the obvious tension in their relationship, Coretta did not neglect her role as a dutiful wife and mother. She was seen packing Martin's clothes for his upcoming trip to Selma, in addition to maintaining the household.

Cadillac Records' (2008) female protagonist, Geneva Wade, also displayed elements of the Black Queen, in addition to providing an implicit connection between womanhood and one's ability to be a mother. She served as a surrogate mother to a younger member of her husband's band, Lil' Walter. She cooked and cleaned for him, and in one scene, she prepared a bath for him. "What you need is a momma, somebody to feed ya, clothe ya, and tell you to get your behind in the bath," Geneva told Lil' Walter.

Her boyfriend, Muddy Waters, seemed to take Geneva's caretaking for granted; later in the movie, Lil' Walter made a pass at Geneva, telling her, "This sure is a nice home you're making, Geneva. Who be takin' care of you? I see you runnin' around here taking care of everybody; who take care of Geneva?" In her loyalty to Muddy, Geneva disregarded Lil' Walter's advances, telling him, "Walter, I'm Muddy's woman. I love him; you have no idea how good that man's been to me. I'm half a woman, Walter. I can't have any more babies; I can't give Muddy any babies of his own." Although she performed the traditional, stereotypical roles of being a woman, she still felt less than, because of her inability to bear children. This statement is important, because Geneva's response connects being considered a "real" woman, to being a mother or having the ability to bear children.

Overall, 42 percent of the characters were supporting roles to their male counterparts, similar to Reid (2004), who stated Black female protagonists' roles are intended to boost the self-esteem of their male counterparts. This also connects with Brooks and Herbert's (2006) evaluation of Spike Lee's female characters in *Bamboozled*, finding those women were defined by the men in their lives. This text supports those findings, as the majority of the women had no identity separate from their husbands and children.

While none of the women in the sample explicitly said they abandoned their professional goals because of their families, it was certainly implied based on their dedication to their husband and responsibility as a mother. Extending this point, Alford et al. (2016) acknowledged there is no comprehensive or monolithic representation of Black women and Black motherhood in television, and this study's sample supports this notion. Many of the mothers in the movies exhibited similar qualities, all of which portray them as a dedicated mother and wife.

Half of the female characters in the sample did not mention working outside of the home, nor were they seen in a work environment. For example, Aretha Cobbs was a quiet, soft-spoken woman who was respected by her husband and members of the community. Aretha was often seen in an apron, wearing pearls, cooking, cleaning and tending to household affairs. She was very accommodating and supportive of her husband and his busy schedule as a pastor, to the point where she supported him kicking their daughter out of their home. Aretha did not have any thoughts independent of her husband in the movie, and when he was not around, her dialogue revolved around their relationship or his actions. She had no independent identity outside of her husband, whom she affectionately referred to as "the Reverend."

Another example was Camille Wright, *Love & Basketball*'s (2000) protagonist's mother. Camille was rarely seen doing non-domestic tasks. She was always wearing an apron and primarily seen carrying laundry, cooking and addressing the domestic needs of her husband and children. Camille often neglected her personal desires to care for her husband and children. In one scene, she told her children how tired she was after cooking and cleaning. Shortly after, her husband entered the room and asked her to iron two shirts for him; while there was slight reluctance, she agreed to the task.

Although on the surface Camille's character appeared to be a housewife, lacking character development and depth, her role provided an insightful juxtaposition to her daughter Monica's character. These contrasting characters illustrated the various dimensions of womanhood. While Monica was assertive and aggressive in maintaining her independence and vocalization against patriarchal dominance, Camille embraced her traditional motherly role, placing the needs of her family before her own. In this mother-daughter relationship, Prince-Bythewood unraveled the conflicting relationships between feminists and anti-feminists. Neither character was depicted as right or wrong, and neither was more of a woman than the other. Aretha, Roz and Camille embraced their role as the Black Queen, despite them not having an identity separate from their families.

All of the female protagonists in the sample were caring and loving toward their partner, contradicting Douglas' (2010) point that Black women are primarily depicted as bossy or unloving. Their portrayals were the exact opposite of the aggressive nature often ascribed to Black women in the media. In fact, half of the characters displayed passive demeanors and characteristics. This contradiction may be a direct attempt from filmmakers to counter common stereotypes often associated with Black women in the media. These filmmakers provided a space of resistance for these characters. However, although these loving and nurturing characteristics contradict common negative behaviors often attributed to Black women in media, their complacency and willingness to accept their partners' indiscretions created an entirely new stereotype uncovered by the researcher: the Dependent Nurturer.

As detailed in previous sections, more than half of the characters in the sample exhibited similar characteristics in the nurturing role they played within their families. They were the dutiful wives, dedicated to rearing their children and supporting their husband's careers and professional ambitions. This unwavering love and support illustrated the bond between these women and their significant other, despite obstacles. From Camille's self-sacrificing behavior in *Love & Basketball* (2000), to Geneva's willingness to raise Muddy's daughter from an outside relationship, these women embraced the wifely submission approach to maintaining their households. Although these were conscious decisions upheld by the women, this passive acceptance and role of the dependent nurturer they played illustrated the lack of agency they held within their relationships.

The love shared between the couples helped sustain their longevity, despite indiscretions and disagreements. The combination of being provided for and unconditional love for their partner not only contributed to the characteristics of the complacent nurturer, but also supported the notion that love conquers all. The ideology of love providing a foundation for relationship survival, regardless of any negative occurrences, was a dominant theme in the movies analyzed, and proved to be consistent with previous scholarship examining romantic relationships in movies (Hefner & Wilson, 2013).

A surface analysis of these women could imply the acceptance of their mate's indiscretions and dependency on their income as a form of weakness, but their ability to remain in the relationship and still provide a loving atmosphere for their children perhaps embodies a strength that is unique to Black women's experiences in a racialized world. Their unwavering support of their partners illustrates Hill and Collins' (1998) notion of undying dedication to their men regardless of their circumstances. In a society that disregards Black bodies, Black women have taken on the responsibility to protect their Black husbands, sons and brothers, even if the circumstances do not reciprocate that appreciation. These cultural experiences of the Black community are not only reflected in these films, but also highlight the continuous struggle to not only define Black Love in a Eurocentric world but create a loving environment that empowers both Black men and women.

References

Alford, A., Maxwell, M., Jones, R., & Morris, A. (2016). Can't have it all: An analysis of black motherhood on reality television. In D. Allison (Ed.), *Black women's portrayals on reality television* (pp. 83–101). Lanham, MD: Lexington Books.

Bobo, J. (1998). *Black women film and video artists.* New York, NY: Routledge.

Bobo, J. (2005). *Black women as cultural readers.* New York, NY: Columbia University Press.

Bogle, D. (2001). *Toms, coons, mulattoes, mammies, and bucks: An interpretive history of blacks in American films.* New York, NY: Bloomsbury Publishing.

Bogle, D. (2007). *Brown sugar: Over one hundred years of America's black female superstars—new expanded and updated edition.* New York, NY: Bloomsbury Academic.

Brock, A., Kvasny, L., & Hales, K. (2010). Cultural appropriations of technical capital: Black women, weblogs, and the digital divide. *Information, Communication & Society, 13*(7), 1040–1059.

Brooks, D. E., & Hébert, L. P. (2006). Gender, race, and media representation. *Handbook of Gender and Communication, 16,* 297–317.

Brown, D. L., White-Johnson, R. L., & Griffin-Fennell, F. D. (2013). Breaking the chains: Examining the endorsement of modern Jezebel images and racial-ethnic esteem among African American women. *Culture, Health & Sexuality, 15*(5), 525–539.

Cartier, N. (2014). Black women on-screen as future texts: A new look at black pop culture representations. *Cinema Journal, 53*(4), 150–157.

Chen, G. M., Williams, S., Hendrickson, N., & Chen, L. (2012). Male mammies: A social-comparison perspective on how exaggeratedly overweight media portrayals of Madea, Rasputia, and Big Momma affect how black women feel about themselves. *Mass Communication and Society, 15*(1), 115–135.

Collins, P. H. (2000). Gender, black feminism, and black political economy. *The Annals of the American Academy of Political and Social Science, 568*(1), 41–53.

Collins, P. H. (2004). *Black sexual politics: African Americans, gender, and the new racism.* New York, NY: Routledge.

Davis, S., & Tucker-Brown, A. (2013). Effects of black sexual stereotypes on sexual decision making among African American women. *Journal of Pan African Studies, 5*(9), 111–129.

Douglas, S. J. (2010). *The rise of enlightened sexism: How pop culture took us from girl power to girls gone wild.* New York, NY: Macmillan.

Eschholz, S., Bufkin, J., & Long, J. (2002). Symbolic reality bites: Women and racial/ethnic minorities in modern film. *Sociological Spectrum, 22*(3), 299–334.

Faluyi, D. (2015). An exploration into the objectification of self in female hip-hop culture as a form of misogyny or empowerment. *Journal of Promotional Communications, 3*(3), 446–464.

Foster, E. (2009). Controlling images of African women: The Hottentot Venus, Alek Wek & the thought of Stuart Hall. *CONCEPT, 33,* 1–13.

Gamson, W. A., Croteau, D., Hoynes, W., & Sasson, T. (1992). Media images and the social construction of reality. *Annual Review of Sociology, 18,* 373–393.

Gibson-Hudson, G. J. (1998). The ties that bind: Cinematic representations by black women filmmakers. *Quarterly Review of Film & Video, 15*(2), 25–44.

Glenn, C. L., & Cunningham, L. J. (2009). The power of black magic: The magical Negro and White salvation in film. *Journal of Black Studies, 40*(2), 135–152.

Harris, T. M., & Hill, P. S. (1998). "Waiting to Exhale" or" Breath (ing) Again": A search for identity, empowerment, and love in the 1990's. *Women and Language, 21,* 9–20.

Hefner, V., & Wilson, B. J. (2013). From love at first sight to soul mate: The influence of romantic ideals in popular films on young people's beliefs about relationships. *Communication Monographs, 80*(2), 150–175.

Hobson, J. (2005). *Venus in the dark: Blackness and beauty in popular culture.* New York, NY: Routledge.

Hooks, B. (1992). *Black looks: Race and representation.* Boston, MA: South End Press.

Hooks, B. (2000). *All about love: New visions.* New York, NY: William Morrow.

Kretsedemas, P. (2010). But she's not black! *Journal of African American Studies, 14*(2), 149–170.

Manatu, N. (2003). *African American women and sexuality in the cinema.* Jefferson, NC: McFarland.

Margolis, H. (1999). Stereotypical strategies: Black film aesthetics, spectator positioning, and self-directed stereotypes in "Hollywood Shuffle" and "I'm Gonna Git You Sucka." *Cinema Journal, 38*(3), 50–66.

Missouri, M. A. (2015). *Black magic woman and narrative film.* New York, NY: Palgrave Macmillan.

Rosenthal, L., & Lobel, M. (2016). Stereotypes of black American women related to sexuality and motherhood. *Psychology of Women Quarterly, 40*(3), 319–336.

Reid, M. A. (2004). *Black lenses, black voices: African American film now.* Lanham, MD: Rowman & Littlefield Publishers.

Reynolds-Dobbs, W., Thomas, K. M., & Harrison, M. S. (2008). From mammy to superwoman images that hinder Black women's career development. *Journal of Career Development, 35*(2), 129–150.

Smith-Shomade, B. E. (2002). *Shaded lives: African-American women and television.* New Brunswick, NJ: Rutgers University Press.

Tyree, T. (2011). African American stereotypes in reality television. *Howard Journal of Communications, 22*(4), 394–413.

Tyree, T. C. (2009). Lovin' momma and hatin' on baby mama: A comparison of misogynistic and stereotypical representations in songs about rappers' mothers and baby mamas. *Women and Language, 32*(2), 50–58.

Tyree, T., & Jones, M. (2015). The adored woman in rap: An analysis of the presence of philogyny in rap music. *Women's Studies, 44*(1), 54–83.

Utley, E. A. (2011). When better becomes worse: Black wives describe their experiences with infidelity. *Black Women, Gender & Families, 5*(1), 68–89.

4 Black Love and Black Feminism

Black Feminist Thought

Enriching media communication research, Black Feminist Thought creates a means for Black women to critically examine how they are represented in the media (Meyers, 2014). The term "Black feminist" has been used to apply to African-American women who possess some version of consciousness (Collins, 1990). Black Feminist Thought takes Elizabeth Cady Stanton's quote, "Prejudice against color ... is no stronger than that against sex" (Chafe, 1977, p. 44) and adds multiple dimensions to analyze the intersectionality between race, gender and class. The theory connects Black female representation with the plight often faced by Black women including racism, sexism, classism and the status of outsider within (Howard-Hamilton, 2003).

Any oppressed group's experiences may put them in a position to see things differently and their lack of control over the hegemonic ideology makes self-definition difficult (Collins, 1989). As Howard-Hamilton (2003) noted, finding theoretical constructs that are appropriate for explaining the experiences of African-American women can be challenging, but Black Feminist Thought highlights the experiences of Black women as unique, which is embedded in the ideology of Blacks in the United States. Black Feminist Thought allows researchers to understand and examine the Black experience from a feminist perspective, combining the fight against sexism with the fight against racism (Brewer, 1999). It represents a second level of knowledge from members who are a part of the oppressed group from their standpoint (Collins, 1989). This view encourages Black women to value their knowledge by including elements and themes of Black women's culture and traditions connecting them with new meaning.

Patricia Hill Collins' Black Feminist Thought included theories or specialized thoughts created by Black women intellectuals in an effort to express a Black woman's standpoint (Collins, 1990). The heart of the Black feminist ideologies is the notion there is a specialized knowledge produced by Black women that illustrates the Black woman's perspective, making these experiences crucial in creating knowledge (Reynolds,

2002). Collins' original theory consisted of three themes, the first stating it is impossible to separate the structure and thematic content of thought from material conditions shaping the lives of its producers. This framework is shaped and produced by the experiences of Black women (Howard-Hamilton, 2003). The second theme claimed Black women possess a unique standpoint shared by other Black women and third, because of the diversity of Black women involving age, class, region and sexual orientation, Black women respond differently to these themes (Collins, 1986; Howard-Hamilton, 2003). Black Feminist Thought encouraged all Black women to create self-definitions validating a Black woman's standpoint and offers them a different view of themselves different from the established social order (Collins, 1989).

In her 1990 book, *Black Feminist Thought: Knowledge, Consciousness, and the Politics of Empowerment*, Collins expanded her theory by detailing additional components. Most relevant to this study is Collins' (1990) notion challenging the controlling images of Black female portrayals as stereotypical mammies, matriarchs, welfare recipients and hot mommas have been essential to dominant ideology that continues to oppress Black women. The controlling images serve as an instrument of power for White men which has been used to keep Black women as an outsider in dominant culture (Collins, 1990). The objectification of Black women as the other does not represent equal relationships and Black Feminist Thought gives a perspective that provides a deeper context and meaning for Black women struggling for a voice (Howard-Hamilton, 2003).

The "outsider within" status that Black women have been ascribed to by the dominant group leaves them invisible with no voice or a sense of belonging (Howard-Hamilton, 2003). Howard-Hamilton (2003) noted Black women will never have a sense of inclusion because of the lack of cultural fit between the experiences of Black women and the dominant group. This lack of space helps create the foundation of Black Feminist Thought that highlights the importance of ideas created by Black women from their perspective.

Connecting Black Feminist Thought to this text, it is important to note Collins' (1990) claim that experiences gained from living as a Black woman in America create a sense of Black feminist consciousness. In turn, this mindfulness influences the Black woman's existence and impacts how she engages with society. These experiences create a "unique angle of vision on self, community and society – and theories that interpret these experiences" (Collins, 1990, p. 22). Supporting this point, hooks (2000a) stated these lived experiences create a different view from those in dominant culture. It is this cultural identity that Gibson-Hudson (1998) noted Black female filmmakers construct images reflective of their uniqueness and historical significance. Missouri (2015) extended this point stating a true Black feminist film addresses Black female subjectivity and issues of social injustice. Additionally, Missouri

(2015) noted that Black women characters should exhibit several qualities including the willingness to fight oppression and imagine possibilities outside of oppressive forces.

Many Black women claim their racial identity is more salient than their gender or class identity, and these factors contribute to how Blacks are perceived in the media (Collins, 1990). Considering this argument, it is vital to examine Black female filmmaker's work in an attempt to highlight reflections of their individual lived experiences as Black women in the characters and narratives they create. The inclusion of the standpoint of oppressed groups is important in creating diverse and inclusive narratives for audience members to be exposed to various cultural experiences. Collins (1990) encouraged Black, female intellectuals to examine all dimensions of a Black woman's standpoint for African-American women; this charge can be applied to the responsibility Black female, filmmakers have in creating images that are reflective of the many dimensions of Black women.

The Black feminist analysis seeks to define and examine the relationship between Black women and political agendas including oppression and resistance strategies (Gibson-Hudson, 1998). Studies (Griffin, 2014; Meyers, 2004) on Black female representation in the media have used Black Feminist Thought to examine how the dominant gaze shapes audience member's understanding of Black femininity. Meyers (2004) used Black Feminist Thought as a framework to examine how race, gender and class intersected to shape the representation of Black women in local television coverage of Freaknik, an annual spring break party in Atlanta. Meyers (2004) found the intersection of race, class and gender minimized the seriousness of violent acts as told through news outlets, and Black women were rarely portrayed as victims associated with these acts. Instead, they were stereotypical Jezebels, who provoked their assaults because of their attire or mere presence at the event (Meyers, 2004). This study noted the complicated relationship between gender, race and class and their link to social consciousness and popular imagery. She said it is important to analyze these intertwined factors to better understand the commonalities existing within a particular race, class or gender (Meyers, 2004).

This study used the intersectionality of race, gender and class to illustrate how these socially constructed categories often dictate the narratives of Black women in media when aligned with dominant ideology.

Gibson-Hudson (1998) offered several principles that guide the Black feminists' analysis of Black women's cinema:

1   Acknowledge that Black women worldwide share a history of patriarchal oppression;
2   Validate Black women's experiences as real and significant;

3 Investigate the cultural history of Black women, including the survival techniques Black women employ to resist oppression and (re)
formulate concepts of womanhood and

4 Acknowledge and respect alternative knowledge systems and the
means by which Black women "recall and recollect" (p. 46).

Similar to Meyers' (2004) application of Black Feminist Thought, as it
relates to representation, Griffin (2014) used the theory to examine how
the White gaze used in *Precious* shaped audience member's understanding of Black femininity. It is through this analysis that Griffin (2014)
suggests the leading protagonist (who is a Black female) appeals to the
light/White characters that often "save" her throughout the course of
movies. Griffin (2014) noted that Black Feminist Thought successfully
undermines the dominant gaze as the definer of oppressed groups.

Griffin's (2014) use of Black Feminist Thought also highlighted the
prevalence of Whiteness, despite the lack of White characters in movies.
Whether we benefit or not, we exist in a society that reproduces race,
class and gender oppressions (Collins, 2016). This observation supports
the notion that dominant ideologies exist in movies, even when Black
characters (and sometimes Black writers and directors) are involved. It
is this same dominant ideology this study will use to examine if Black
female writers and directors follow these narratives or if they create a
place of self-definition and self-valuation as defined in Black Feminist
Thought.

Survival for Black women is contingent on their ability to find a
place to describe their experiences (Howard-Hamilton, 2003), and as
Collins (1990) noted, Black Feminist Thought can help create a collective identity among African-American women embodying the varying
dimensions of Black women's identity. Black female filmmakers have the
opportunity to create a consciousness that contradicts the stereotypical
images often associated with Black women in movies. It is important to
note that Black Feminist Thought cannot combat race, gender and class
oppression without empowering African-American women (Collins,
1990), which is why this theory's application to this text is imperative
in examining how Black female filmmakers use their narratives to either
empower or oppress the characters they develop. Women are subordinate to men, yet the pecking order between Black and White women
creates hegemonic, marginalized and subordinated femininities; in this
context Black femininity is subordinated in its relation to White women
(Collins, 2004).

The theory's core theme of controlling images and Black women's oppression help guide this research in understanding how the perspective of
Black female filmmakers could potentially counter the controlling images
often associated with Black women in the media. Collins (1990) specifically identifies media as an essential agency critical in transforming the

oppressive images of Black women. Although the media perpetuates the oppressive images of women, it is necessary for Blacks to take control of the images and narratives seen in the media. Solidarity among Black women's narratives is essential in creating a voice for the Black woman's position which should construct, affirm and maintain a dynamic standpoint, (Collins, 1996). In her article, "Learning from the outsider within: The sociological significance of Black feminist thought," Collins (1986) highlighted literary pieces created by Black women that serve as a source of self-definition and self-valuation of Black women. This point emphasized the importance of Black women creating their own narratives in order to help shape the discourse of understanding Black women.

Black Feminism and Black Love

Despite scholars and Black female filmmakers noting the responsibility Black female filmmakers have in creating movies that embody Black feminist ideals, 5 of the 18 characters in the sample explicitly embodied characteristics consistent with Black Feminist Thought. Monica in *Love & Basketball* (2002), Kenya McQueen in *Something New* (2006), Etta James in *Cadillac Records* (2008), Noni Jean in *Beyond the Lights* (2014) and Belle have small moments in their movies where they address patriarchal oppression.

Collins' (1990) Black Feminist Thought provided a framework for analysis for the movies under sample. The idea that Black women share a unique standpoint that should fight patriarchal oppression, empower Black women and challenge controlling images are all concepts that scholars (Howard-Hamilton, 2003; Missouri, 2015) claim should be included in Black feminist films. Although these shared lived experiences described by hooks (2000a) provided a different view from dominant culture, the experiences portrayed in these movies did not illustrate a collective Black woman's experience that could be empowering for Black female audiences. Unfortunately, few of the movies in the sample embodied Gibson-Hudson's (1998) elements analysis for Black Feminist films:

> 1) Acknowledge that Black women worldwide share a history of patriarchal oppression; 2) Validate Black women's experiences as real and significant; 3) Investigate the cultural history of Black women, including the survival techniques Black women employ to resist oppression and (re)formulate concepts of womanhood and 4) Acknowledge and respect alternative knowledge systems and the means by which Black women "recall and recollect."
>
> (p. 46)

In a conversation with Quincy, Monica, a superstar basketball player in *Love & Basketball* (2000), discussed the double standard in sports.

She told Quincy, who also plays basketball, "you jump up in some guy's face, you talk smack and you get a pat on your ass. But because I'm a female, I get told to calm down and act like a lady. I'm a ball player." This statement highlighted the patriarchal dominance and acceptance in sports supported by Gibson-Hudson's (1998) guiding principles. Director, Prince-Bythewood, used people's responses to Monica's tomboy demeanor to illustrate how anything not traditionally feminine is considered different or out of the norm. Monica's character was the embodiment of controlling negative images.

Monica often criticized her mother for being prissy, expressing her discontent in a pivotal scene where she confronted her mother for sacrificing herself for the sake of her family. Monica said to her mother,

> You never stand up for yourself. What's crazy is you not being a caterer so your husband can feel like a man knowing his wife is home cooking and ironing his drawers. If I was ashamed, it was because of that.

Her mother explained to Monica that it was an honor for her to have been able to provide her family with three meals a day and a clean house. Camille's explanation highlighted the belief that for some, being a wife and mom supersede everything else and embodied her definition of Black Love.

Throughout *Love & Basketball* (2002) Monica struggled to connect with her mother, who was the exact opposite of her – girly and prissy. Their relationship provided two perspectives of womanhood. Her mother could be described as anti-feminist because of her dedication to her husband and her role as a homemaker, while Monica's assertiveness could be described as the typical feminist because of her opposition to traditional roles relegated women. Both characters were comfortable in their defined space of womanhood and director Prince-Bythewood strategically juxtaposed the characters to illustrate the multiple identities Black women can embody. Although Camille did not directly fight patriarchal oppression or display concern with social justice and political activism, her comfort within her decision to be a housewife exhibits an entirely new element of Black feminism. Instead of asserting herself to overtly challenge controlling and negative images, she asserts her agency with her decision power, a choice that many Black women traditionally did not have. Her willingness to give up her career to take care of the well-being of her husband and children is remarkably feminist. She is empowered and fulfilled in her role as a stay-at-home wife and that depiction of Black women's experiences is rarely portrayed in Hollywood, especially not from a feminist perspective. Camille's character allowed director Prince-Bythewood to depict the multiple dimensions of Black feminism.

Monica's display of Black feminism in the film exhibits themes more closely related to Black women's struggle to find balance in love and their career. Over the course of the film, we see Monica grapple with embracing her career as basketball player, while creating her definition of womanhood. It is apparent early in the film that Camille wanted Monica to be more ladylike and act like a "girl" was supposed to, although Monica displayed no intentions of conforming to societies standards of womanhood. Early scenes in the film show Camille attempt to make Monica behave more ladylike, telling her, "Monica, sit still. And don't sit on your knees; you'll turn them black." In later scenes, Camille said she would be glad when Monica outgrew her tomboy phase; however, Monica was more interested in honing her skills on the court than wearing a dress. Her mother seemed most proud of her in the few instances where Monica embraced the traditional female characteristics, telling her the night of her prom, "I just want you to enjoy being beautiful." Monica conforms to the stereotypical standards of beauty and in as much resistance as she displayed preparing for the prom putting on makeup and wearing a form-fitting dress, there were also moments where she embraced the ultra-feminine culture. In the moment where she looks at herself in the mirror before leaving, there was a slight grin on her face, perhaps happy that she could conform to society's standards even just for a moment. Camille's character embodies the rhetoric of beauty expectations and Prince-Bythewood used that to expose the many ways beauty could be displayed. Although Monica was never considered beautiful during her games, or wearing jeans and a T-shirt, this scene was pivotal because of its transformative narrative. That night, Monica lost her virginity to Quincy, solidifying her induction into womanhood.

When the couple decided to attend University of Southern California, both on basketball scholarships, Monica continued to figure out her definition of womanhood and how they would be reflected in her basketball career and relationship with Quincy. This balance reached a critical point when Quincy learned about his father's infidelities as previously described. After Monica decided to adhere to her team's curfew instead of comforting Quincy, he grew emotionally distant, ultimately ending their relationship. Her decision, while minor, was reflective of the conflict many Black women are confronted with – supporting your significant other and/or children, oftentimes sacrificing their careers and personal preference for the well-being of others.

MONICA: That night you wanted to talk about your dad I had a curfew. What was I supposed to do?
QUINCY: Stay!
MONICA: If I stayed, I wouldn't be starting!
QUINCY: Least you got your priorities straight.

MONICA: I never asked you to choose.
QUINCY: Never had to.
MONICA: I'm a ballplayer. If anyone knows what that means it should be you.

In this moment, Monica was torn between her two loves and forced to choose and either decision would have compromised her success as an athlete and her love for Quincy. Monica was no longer able to balance her two worlds, thus altering her identity and perspective of womanhood.

Beyonce Knowles Carter's portrayal of Etta James in *Cadillac Records* (2008) displayed a strong, assertive personality. As previously discussed, Etta made a few statements in the movies addressing not only issues of race, but also issues of systematic oppression of the Black woman. She seemed to recognize the power of her talent and she used that as a means of survival, despite the system that was designed to dominate her. After Leonard's multiple attempts to "take care" of Etta, she told him, "I don't need no man to take care of me." James understood her power to create a livelihood for herself without depending on the support from a man, especially a White man. While this independence was not latent throughout her character's depiction in the movie, it served as a subtle reminder of Etta's acknowledgment and understanding of the world around her.

Despite James' financial difficulties and personal struggles with addiction that played out through the film, her character was very cognizant in her role as a Black entertainer in the Jim Crow Era. After Chess learns about James facing foreclosure, he volunteers to buy her home, allowing her to retain residency. Despite her desperation, James voiced her opposition:

CHESS: Come on! I ain't takin' from you, I'm offering!
JAMES: What the fuck is "us"? A White man and a Black girl? I been there.

This scene illustrates James' acknowledgment of Black women's oppression, supporting Griffin's (2004) characteristics of a Black Feminist film. James maintained a powerful voice throughout the film, using it to illustrate her definition of love. James fought to maintain her independence throughout the film and there was no hesitation in her outward expression of Black women's oppression.

Much like James, Kenya McQueen's character in *Something New* (2006) exhibited characteristics consistent with Black Feminist Thought as it related to her career as a senior accountant at a prestigious L.A. Firm. As the only Black woman shown in her work environment, McQueen was often second-guessed by her White male client,

Jack Pino. During meetings with him, Pino would request validation from McQueen's White male superior, oftentimes outwardly dissenting against McQueen's recommendation for his account. When McQueen shared her frustration with her White boyfriend, Brian Kelly, she described her experiences as a part of the "Black Tax," a notion that Black people must work harder in corporate environments to appear competent to their White peers. In a separate conversation with Kelly after experiencing another condescending meeting with Pino, McQueen and Kelly had a critical conversation that highlighted their lack of understanding of one another in their romantic relationship and many tenants of Black Feminist Thought and the patriarchal oppression many Black women face in the workforce:

MCQUEEN: The White boys at the plantation are getting on my last nerves.

KELLY: Can we put the White boys on hold for tonight?

MCQUEEN: What are you saying?

KELLY: Just not tonight, babe. I had a rough day, too. I need to get home and relax.

MCQUEEN: You're asking me to not talk about race?... You expect me to be in this relationship with you and never bring it up?

KELLY: We talk about it all the time. I just said, not right now.

MCQUEEN: When? When is appropriate? When we're at home behind closed doors and we're just joking about it?

KELLY: Just not all the time, it just makes me feel uncomfortable. I'm sorry I wasn't brought up that way.

MCQUEEN: You don't have to talk about being White because no one reminds you every day that you're White. The only times you guys know you're White is when you're in a room full of Black people. I'm in a room full of White people and every day they remind me that I'm Black...

Kelly interrupted, reminding her of her status of an account manager at a large White firm, her salary and her education achievements as a top graduate of Stanford University and Wharton Business School. Kelly's comments provide an interesting juxtaposition to McQueen's argument, highlighting how Black women's oppression is often overlooked because of materialistic success, dictated by accolades. McQueen, however, counters Kelly, arguing that despite her professional achievements, she still has to fight against discrimination.

When I show up at an account meeting, they always have to regroup when they find out I'm the one that's responsible for their multi-million-dollar acquisition. They'd rather trust it to a file clerk ... because he's White! Do you know how insulting that is?

When Kelly responded by telling her he simply wanted a night off from discussing race-related issues, McQueen said, "That's what being Black is about, Brian. You don't get a night off."

As previously mentioned, McQueen and Kelly's race was a major factor in their romantic relationship and this scene illustrated its influence on McQueen's ability to feel understood within her relationship. This open acceptance and acknowledgment of Black American's struggle with oppressive ideologies has proven to be a critical facet of Black Love depictions in Hollywood and is this validation of a shared experience that contributes to the resistance Black couples have historically endured as a unit (hooks, 2000b). The disagreement between McQueen and Kelly perhaps highlights a fundamental distinction between Black Love and Eurocentric-centered love.

This conversation also highlighted Black women's experiences as a collective and it also illustrated the White ignorance that exists related to Black women's experiences in the workforce (Collins, 2004). McQueen's acknowledgment of Black woman's oppression and her fight against dominant ideologies solidified her character as a true Black feminist. Although she never voiced these concerns at work, her dedication to her career was evident and supported by her White male supervisor who acknowledged the undermining behavior from Pino. While viewers may have expected or even hoped McQueen spoke out against Pino directly, her professional and respectful response highlighted the lived experiences of many Black professional women. Although many women may experience similar examples of disrespect or discrimination in the workforce, it often goes unaddressed out of fear of losing employment or being labeled the "angry Black woman," a stereotype that has plagued Black women's identity in the workforce (Stephens & Phillips, 2003). Optimistically, despite the challenges McQueen encountered, she was named partner at the end of the film, a fairy tale ending that many Black women, like her, have to fight for in their reality.

Also consistent with Black feminism, McQueen's character and her girlfriends challenged negative and controlling images by addressing the superwoman stereotype, a depiction that portrays professionally successful, educated Black women as unable to maintain romantic relationships because of their dedication to their careers (Reynolds-Dobbs, Thomas, & Harrison, 2008; Stephens & Phillips, 2003). This notion was specifically addressed in an early scene in the film where McQueen was sharing Valentine's Day dinner with her three closest friends – Cheryl, a judge, Nedra, a banker and Suzette, a pediatrician. During the conversation, Suzette mentioned an article stating 42.4 percent of Black women never get married and most of those women are African-American, educated professionals. In true hopeless-romantic fashion, McQueen responded saying, "I'm just tired of being classified as the victim. Single, Black professional woman destined to be unhappy and alone...." In that brief statement, McQueen outright challenged the notion that Black women are hopelessly doomed to a life of loneliness simply because they are professionally successful. Many scholars (Bobo, 2005; Reynolds-Dobbs et al., 2008) have highlighted how the media often perpetuates this stereotype, rarely offering a counterimage that suggests successful Black women are capable of finding and achieving love. *Something New* (2006) counters these claims not only through the main character's experiences, but also subsequently through her friend's romantic relationships. These depictions may provide comfort to Black female audiences, debunking the myth that Black women must sacrifice their careers in order to find love (or vice versa).

In the 18th-century drama depicting a biracial woman's quest to abolish British slavery, the protagonist, Belle, progressed into womanhood all while acknowledgment of her role within a very segregated London. She understood that women were property of their husbands and family, and she also acknowledged that her biracial background and gender solidified her social standing as inferior. She told her potential suitor,

> [I]t came to my head that I've been blessed with freedom twice over. As a negro and as a woman. Must not a lady marry even if she's financially secure. Who is she without a husband of consequence? Seems silly; like a free negro who begs for a master.

Despite the standards determined by society during that era, Belle associated freedom as a woman with financial independence, also illustrating her recognition of patriarchal oppression and Black women's oppression from the White patriarchal ideologies.

After rejecting Oliver Ashford's request for marriage, in a defining moment in the film, Belle defends herself against Ashford's mother who attempted to shame her:

> ... but [your tongue] explains well enough why I may not marry your son. You see my circumstances as unfortunate, though I cannot carry the same unfortunate as those who share my color. My greatest misfortune would be to join a family that carries me as their shame. As I have been required to carry my own mother, her apparent crime to be born Negro. Am I to be the evidence? I wish to deny her no more than I wish to deny myself. You would pardon me for wanting a husband who feels forgiveness of my bloodline is unnecessary and without grace.

This scene is perhaps among the most important in the film, as it established

Belle's feminist stance and validation of her Black womanhood. Collins (1993) noted Black feminism as a tool that cultivates a fundamental paradigm shift in how people think about oppression; Belle's proclamation illustrated this shift in thinking. Her desperation of acceptance and love was immediately removed in this moment in her rejection of oppression. This narrative shift highlighted critical and reflective thinking about race and gender, challenging the discourse within popular culture (Reynolds, 2002).

Beyond the Lights' (2014) Noni Jean's sexualized lyrics, clothing and persona exhibited characteristics of the Jezebel, combined with typical characteristics of the Tragic Mulatto defined Jean's depiction in the early portion of the film. As she evolved as an artist and asserted her independence against her management, Jean empowered herself by fighting patriarchal images and challenging her previous negative image. It is Jean's depiction in this film that provided an unlikely glimpse of Black feminism. For example, when Jean and Nicol travel to Mexico to escape the demands of Jean's image and profession, she literally and figuratively removes her persona and evolves from being a sexualized spectacle, to a woman asserting her agency over her career and personal relationships. She was no longer portrayed strictly as a sexual being as Brooks and Herbet (2006) noted, but evolved as a romantic interest for her counterpart, Nicol.

The hypersexuality and exploitation of Jean and her talent symbolically illustrated the role of Black women in the media and music industry in today's society. For example, in describing Jean's image, her mother/ manager said, "We're selling a fantasy." That fantasy included posing nearly naked for magazine covers and singing sexually explicit lyrics. The depicted commodification of Black women's talent and beauty has been discussed by countless researchers (Collins, 2004; hooks, 2000; Manatu, 2003) and Prince-Bythewood highlighted these trends through Jean's characterization. She was powerless in making important career decisions; her image was manufactured for her, not to highlight her undeniable talent, but to objectify her body for the financial gain of her mother/manager and record label. Jean's willingness to conform to society's standards of sexualized Black womanhood and femininity illustrates Collins' notion of controlling images that serve as ideological justification for the material violence aimed at Black women (Peoples, 2007). Contemporary sexual politics in America ignore Black people, oftentimes depicting them as an afterthought; there is only a slight deviation when Black women are depicted sexually, as an ornament or decoration in a scene (Collins, 2004).

Materialistic, sexualized Black women became a theme in hip-hop culture, subjecting women to degrading and oppressive images (Collins, 2004; Stephens & Phillips, 2003). These depictions invoke historical meanings of Black female sexuality, elevating the politics of race and sexuality (Collins, 2004). Jean's biracial background adds another dimension to her characterization, as light-skinned and biracial women have historically been portrayed as oversexualized women in conflict because of their mixed race. The biracial or Tragic Mulatto's characteristics include physical beauty, sensuality, mental instability and an inability to escape her disastrous life created because of her Blackness – all of which serve as historical evidence or racism in today's world (Perkins, 2005).

Although masked as a woman in control of her sexuality and image, Jean was visibly uncomfortable with her sexual image and the direction of her career. It was not until the film's climax, Jean willingly accepted and embodied the stereotypical images used to shape her career within the industry. These images, according to Collins (2004), manufacture consent for domination forcing Black women to accept subordinate place within society. However, Prince-Bythewood's depiction of Jean as a sexy, pop culture icon highlights these common portrayals of Black women in the music industry and media, yet her transformation juxtaposes these portrayals, establishing her agency and fight against stereotypically oppressive images. When Jean reaches her breaking point, yelling at her mother, "I am not a bloody product," her self-actualization rejects the negative images formerly forced on her. Noni Jean's character was a symbol of a feminist transformation.

Despite the liberating enlightenment Jean experienced in the film, I would be remiss to not recognize that this insightfulness was facilitated by her relationship with Nicol. He challenged her to honor her voice and desires for her career and he also provided a safe space for her vulnerability. As she was embracing her newly found liberation in a conversation with Nicol, Jean said, "Everybody says I'm special cause I have this voice but I'm just saying what everybody else wants me to say. I need to say something." Perhaps Jean would have embraced her natural beauty, rejected her hair extensions, excessive make-up and revealing clothes without meeting Nicol, but his character served as a rhetorical tool of reflection and accountability Jean needed to progress forward. Nicol's role in Jean's transformation was perhaps a flaw in the film's depiction of feminist principles. Ironically, Jean was encouraged to challenge the negative images she was subjected to with the assistance of a man, not straying far from common Hollywood narratives that women are incapable of making major decisions without the facilitation of a man. Perhaps Prince-Bythewood used their relationship to exemplify an important element of Black Love – the reciprocal support that aid in allowing each person to become the best versions of themselves exemplifying the perfect balance between Black feminism and Black Love.

Although none of the movies in the sample portrayed women as single mothers, this dysfunctional familial system illustrated in many of the relationships supports Collins' (1998) notion that Black family values are weakening, primarily because of their deteriorating family structure. The ideal family structure is defined as a father who is head of the household, mother and children connected through an emotional bond and mutual love (Collins, 1998). Collins (1998) noted feminist scholarship challenged this understanding of the nuclear family by discrediting this consideration as normalcy. As previously stated, a Black feminist film should empower Black women and challenge negative images, especially as it relates to depictions of families and romantic relationships. However, the majority of these films do not support that ideology, instead they relegate the mother's role strictly to the house. Black women can never fully be empowered in the contexts that harms Black men (Collins, 2004). The portrayals of the traditional family ideal where men work and women stay at home reify several types of oppression (Collins, 2000). Not only do these movies counter the essence of a Black feminist film, but they depict the Black family's foundation as weak and dysfunctional.

New knowledge about their own experiences can be empowering and allow subordinate groups to define and create their own reality (Collins, 1993). The power of self-definition speaks to the importance of Black feminism, placing consciousness on African-American women. The characteristics of Black Feminism were often exhibited in these films, specifically connected to the character's romantic relationships. Perhaps addressing patriarchal oppression is an essential element of Black Love, thus adding another component to the concept's nuanced definition. These characters were only free to display their opposition to oppression within their romantic relationships, which served as a safe place for these women to challenge the oppression they faced in other elements of their lives.

References

Bobo, J. (2005). *Black women as cultural readers*. New York, NY: Columbia University Press.

Brewer, R. (1999). Theorizing race, class and gender: The new scholarship of black feminist intellectuals and black women's labor. In Brewer, R. (Eds). *Race, Gender & Class* (pp. 29–47). New York, NY: Routledge.

Brooks, D. E., & Hébert, L. P. (2006). Gender, race, and media representation. *Handbook of Gender and Communication, 16*, 297–317.

Chafe, W. H. (1977). *Women and equality: Changing patterns in American culture*. New York, NY: Oxford University Press.

Collins, P. H. (1986). Learning from the outsider within: The sociological significance of black feminist thought. *Social Problems, 33*(6), S14–S32.

Collins, P. H. (1989). The social construction of black feminist thought. *Signs, 14*(4), 745–773.

Collins, P. H. (1990). *Black feminist thought: Knowledge, consciousness, and the politics of empowerment*. New York, NY: Routledge.

Collins, P. H. (1993). Black feminist thought in the matrix of domination. In Lemert, C. (Ed.) *Social theory: The multicultural and classic readings* (pp. 615–625). New York, NY: Routledge.

Collins, P. H. (2004). *Black sexual politics: African Americans, gender, and the new racism*. New York, NY: Routledge.

Collins, P. H. (2016). Toward a new vision: Race, class, and gender as categories of analysis and connection. In Brewer, R. (Eds). *Race, Gender and Class* (pp. 65–75). New York, NY: Routledge.

Gibson-Hudson, G. J. (1998). The ties that bind: Cinematic representations by black women filmmakers. *Quarterly Review of Film & Video, 15*(2), 25–44.

Griffin, R. A. (2014). Pushing into precious: Black women, media representation, and the glare of the White supremacist capitalist patriarchal gaze. *Critical Studies in Media Communication, 31*(3), 182–197.

hooks, B. (2000a). *Feminist theory: From margin to center*. London: Pluto Press.

hooks, B. (2000b). *All about love: New visions*. New York, NY: William Morrow.

Howard-Hamilton, M. F. (2003). Theoretical frameworks for African American women. *New Directions for Student Services, 2003*(104), 19–27.

Meyers, M. (2004). African American women and violence: Gender, race, and class in the news. *Critical Studies in Media Communication, 21*(2), 95–118.

Missouri, M. A. (2015). *Black magic woman and narrative film*. New York, NY: Palgrave Macmillan.

Peoples, W. A. (2007). "Under construction": Identifying foundations of hip-hop feminism and exploring bridges between Black second-wave and hip-hop feminisms. *Meridians: Feminism, Race, Transnationalism, 8*(1), 19–52.

Perkins, M. (2005). Thoroughly modern Mulatta: Rethinking "Old World" stereotypes in a "New World" setting. *Biography, 28*(1), 104–116.

Reynolds, T. (2002). Re-thinking a black feminist standpoint. *Ethnic and Racial Studies, 25*(4), 591–606.

Reynolds-Dobbs, W., Thomas, K. M., & Harrison, M. S. (2008). From mammy to superwoman images that hinder Black women's career development. *Journal of Career Development, 35*(2), 129–150.

Stephens, D. P., & Phillips, L. D. (2003). Freaks, gold diggers, divas, and dykes: The sociohistorical development of adolescent African American women's sexual scripts. *Sexuality and Culture, 7*(1), 3–49.

Conclusion

Hollywood narratives have created a system of knowledge that reinforces White patriarchal hegemony, while oppressing minorities in an effort to maintain White supremacy (hooks, 2003). Women and minorities have fought for positive and accurate representation in Hollywood since its inception, but the lack of diversity both behind and in front of the camera has hindered the ability to change the stereotypical narratives ascribed to individuals in those demographics. Negative portrayals are influenced by our nation's racialized structure, and oftentimes they reflect the ideologies and beliefs of those creating the narratives (Smith, 2013).

Through an examination of Hollywood movies directed by Black women, this text found that despite diverse representation behind the camera, many of the narratives did not promote empowering reflections of Black women, specifically as it related to romantic relationships or Black Love. Overall, the women in the sample did not embody many elements of stereotypes often associated with Black women in the media, but there were traces of a contemporary version of the Tragic Mulatto stereotype and the depiction of a new stereotype, the dependent nurturer. This study also found Black romantic relationships embody bell hooks' (2000) characteristics of love more than Hendrick and Hendrick's (1986) Six Love Styles. The most consistent themes among the relationships were issues of infidelity and women's acceptance of these indiscretions, which were elements of the dependent nurturer's characteristics. It is important to note that 5 of the 12 movies were based on true stories or play adaptations, illustrating not only the lack of creative freedom and license, but also the limited opportunities afforded to Black women in Hollywood. Even when they are given the opportunity to serve in pivotal behind-the-scenes roles, Black female filmmakers are still controlled by the constraints of creating a story shaped by someone else's narrative.

hooks (2000) argued Black romantic relationships are portrayed as unloving, and those within the relationship as unlovable. However, this study found the women in the sample were not portrayed as unloving; rather, they displayed unconditional love in an effort to maintain the harmony within their families. Black women were not depicted as overly sexual, unloving, aggressive bitches. In fact, they were portrayed as nurturing, loving and caretakers, roles Black women have fought for since the beginning of media.

Many of the characters sampled exhibited qualities of the Black Queen, depicted as motherly, nurturing and held in high regard in the Black community (Tyree, 2009). These women were supportive of their husbands and sacrificed many of their personal desires for the sake of their families. Many of the women in the sample embodied the ideals of traditional White womanhood, displaying themselves as poised homemakers only concerned with maintaining the appearance of a successful relationship. The combination of these characteristics with their acceptance of their significant other's infidelities points to the dependent nurturer.

These findings also supported the notion that "love conquers all." Based on this study's findings, "Black Love" is defined as a mutually beneficial relationship, based on acceptance and the sharing of resources that enable the family's survival. Although Black Love is revered on social media as goals people aspire to attain, ironically, that same admiration and positive reflection is rarely seen in Hollywood. If this study's findings are true, Black Love from a woman's perspective is the acceptance of disrespectful behavior. Most of the couples in this sample did not illustrate a relationship reflective of mutual respect, unconditional love and support. Instead, it was an illustration of women's inability to assert themselves against the wrongdoings inflicted on them from their partners. Additionally, these women were dependent on their significant others to maintain their lifestyle.

The combination of the themes found in the sample, the roles ascribed to the characters and the way love was displayed illustrated a representation of Black women's love experiences in Hollywood movies. The Dependent Nurturer was content within her dysfunctional relationship and accepts her husband's disloyalty, because he demonstrated his love for her by providing for their family. It is the connection between each of these dynamics that create consistent themes of Black Love in the movies examined.

Although this text acknowledged the agency Black women hold behind the scenes to counter negative stereotypes often associated with Black women in the media, these findings also revealed the perhaps unintentional creation of a new stereotype. The Dependent Nurturer was a consistent stereotype among the characters examined. She was a loving, motherly and nurturing caretaker, despite her husband's unfaithfulness. Even if she knew about her significant other's infidelities, she accepted his actions because of his role as the primary breadwinner of the household and to also maintain their coveted social status by embracing respectability politics and negotiate the relationship between bitchiness, promiscuity and fertility as Collins (2004) noted. The dependent nurturer embodied characteristics of the Black Queen, a woman who is held in high regard within the community, but her willingness to sacrifice her personal desires, combined with her contentment within her dysfunctional relationship, created an entirely new archetype of Black women's representation in the media.

Combining these depictions with their romantic relationships, many of these characters lacked the true embodiment of love. While they provided unconditional love to their partners and children, there were many cases in this sample where that same dedication was not reciprocated in their relationships. Black women are often the ones who bear the brunt of Black men's anger and continue to operate so thoroughly through gendered practices and ideologies (Collins, 2004) which were evident in these character's actions. Perhaps the Black female filmmaker was illustrating the burden of the Black woman, maintaining the household and rearing the children, all while upholding dignity even after knowing about their husband's infidelities. Portraying Black women as passive stifles the notions that Black women can actively change their circumstances; similarly, presenting Black women as heroes fosters the perception that Black women need no help (Collins, 1993). Black women are often depicted as strong and enduring, rarely displaying evidence of working through issues they are confronted with. They are rarely shown processing or working through their issues, instead they move forward without dealing with their emotions. As seen in these films, the authenticity of Black women's experiences is often based on notions of suffering, dysfunction and marginalization of Black women (Reynolds, 2002).

This ideal of the Black woman who can endure hurt and trauma without being impacted is unrealistic and perhaps one of the most prevalent characteristics associated with Black women on screen. In reality, Black women choose to support Black men at all costs, whether granting sexual favors, ignoring Black male abuse or caring for their children. Black women have learned to become the Strong Black Woman, which ultimately means enduring abuse. For many Black women, motherhood has become the primary site where the Strong Black Woman holds rank and Black motherhood remains valued by the majority of Black women; it is through motherhood that Black women exercise strength, demonstrate power and often suffer the consequences (Collins, 2004). These notions were evident throughout the themes of these films.

Based on the characteristics associated with Black feminist films and this study's findings, almost half of Black female directors displayed elements of Black feminism. Supporting Gibson-Hudson (1998), many of the Black female filmmakers in this sample presented diverse images of Black womanhood, while others reiterated the same types of imagery for each of these characters and, in subtle ways, reinforced the ideologies of the dominant culture. The filmmakers incorporated elements of images commonly accepted among audience members, which, unfortunately, are problematic for Black women. This study, however, did not find any overt challenges to the misrepresentations of Black women in the media, thus contesting the notion that Black female filmmakers create narratives resisting the objectification of dominant culture.

Although these narratives that did not include feminist themes were not consistent with traditional negative stereotypes of Black women in the media, they still were not feminist movies as described by Gibson-Hudson (1998) or Collins (1990). Combining Gibson-Hudson's (1998) principles of Black women's cinema with Collins' (1990) themes of Black Feminist Thought, 58 percent of the movies examined did not exhibit any of the defined characteristics. In those films, there was very little or no mention of the Black women's experience as a collective unit, patriarchal oppression or challenges to controlling images. Although these experiences may vary, Collins (2016) argued that one commonality exists among Black women – the negative effects of race, class and gender oppression simultaneously. With these basic elements of Black feminism missing from these movies, there seems to be a lack of representation of true Black feminism is lacking in Hollywood, even when Black women are creating the narratives. There is still a void for media that empowers and liberates Black female audience members, and if those positive messages do not come from Black women, one must ask, where will they come from?

Scholars have noted movies as a source of liberation and expression for minority filmmakers, especially Black women (Collins, 1990; Gibson-Hudson, 1998). Yet, as this study found, Black female directors are clearly relegated to upholding consistent narratives that prevent their true ability to exercise their voice and agency. While previous scholarship acknowledges the constraints Hollywood places on the types of narratives that are accepted, researchers have suggested diversification both behind and in front of the camera would contribute to more positive and comprehensive portrayals of minorities (Erigha, 2014). This study revealed the extreme limitations and standards Black filmmakers are held to. Although the filmmakers in the sample did not display stereotypes perpetuated in movies created by men, similar to Williams (2015) findings, this study noted the difference in the portrayal of women in films created by women.

Although the dependent nurturer countered the ideologies consistent with Black feminist films noted by previous scholars, these Black female filmmakers did not depict the adoption of the traditional motherly roles as negative or anti-feminist. While some of the female characters in the movies did not assert their agency against controlling images, acknowledge Black women's oppression or use their position to empower Black women, they still coveted their role as a mother, housewife and primary caregiver for their families. This embracement of traditional characteristics of a woman's role could be considered a new element of Black feminism. Although they were not overtly demonstrating resistance against patriarchal ideologies, the acceptance of their role spoke to the freedom, however limited, Black women have in choosing whether to uphold traditional values or challenge oppressive images.

Black Love Depictions' Influence on Viewers

These narratives have significant impact on how Black romantic relationships are portrayed in the media, which ultimately could affect and influence audience members. Media effects research has linked media content with behavior of audiences, specifically as it relates to romantic relationships (Haferkamp, 1999). In her analysis of audience members' viewing habits of soap operas and their attitudes about dysfunctional relationships, Haferkamp (1999) found audiences who viewed negative content often ascribed similar behavior to their relationships. If Kaferkamp's (1999) findings hold true, this is particularly problematic for this study's findings. Considering the majority of the themes found in this sample exhibited an overwhelming amount of infidelity and mistrust in romantic relationships, Kaferkamp's (1999) study would imply audiences adopt this behavior in their romantic relationships. Instead of loving relationships as defined by hooks (2000), Black romantic relationships are subjected to lying, cheating and women neglecting themselves and their personal desires.

While previous research has expressed the necessity of diverse representation in Hollywood in front and behind the camera to create positive, non-stereotypical images of minorities, this text found that despite having Black women drive the narratives and imagery in movies, they still follow the disconfirming script of minority representation in Hollywood, such as the dependent nurturer. This could mean Black women do not experience loving relationships in their lives, thus these movies are a representation of their lived experiences, or Black filmmakers create narratives that are consistent with negative ideologies often associated with minorities in an effort to have their content accepted by the masses. Either conclusion proves to be problematic for the argument of diversifying Hollywood.

According to Hall's notion of visual representation, images in the media serve as a production of identity rather than a reflection of fixed historical and cultural truths of the African Diaspora (Missouri, 2015). In other words, what we see produces our identity, versus our identity impacting and influencing what we see. How individuals construct their social identities is shaped by commodified texts produced by the media that are segmented by the social constructions of race and gender. Essentially, media are central to what represents our social realities (Brooks & Hebert, 2006). The media play a vital role in shaping our gendered and racialized media culture, in turn cultivating socialization (Brooks & Hebert, 2006). Perhaps filmmakers should consider shifting the narratives they create to include more loving and nurturing relationships.

Holding true to media effects, this change could potentially impact Black romantic relationships more positively, thus contributing to more positive and functional Black romantic relationships. The Black filmmaker must depict an authentic reflection of Black life in America, while being inextricably tied to commercialized sensibilities of a mass audience that is either avoiding or denying the truth (Guerrero, 1993). Filmmakers can create the most liberating filmic vision related to the diaspora, but if it does not find an audience, it will have little social impact.

These stories aimed to define the Black experience, but audience members must understand these perspectives are not reflective of what all Black women feel. Films that are generally accepted and financed in Hollywood often depict family or relationship breakdown, creating a one-dimensional view of Black women's experiences (Reynolds, 2002). Blackness is a social construct informed by historical, cultural and political variations that cannot be isolated to accommodate dominant ideologies. It has different meanings for different audience members that are combined with passion, spiritual awareness and emotional sensibilities (Staples, 2005). Each individual has a unique personal experience made up of values, motivations and emotions. Human connections can be freeing and empowering, as is the case with Black women's romantic relationships (Collins, 1993). The emotional and physical abuse that Black women often experience from their fathers, lovers and husbands reflects practices that oppose feminists' values, yet they are often affirmed by those same feminists to reinforce Black culture and traditions (Collins, 1993).

Erigha (2018) noted because Black directors are so few in Hollywood, they are often unable to penetrate Hollywood studios without subscribing to those dominant ideologies; this text supports this notion, finding Black female directors subscribe to stereotypical roles, perhaps to be accepted by Hollywood. If filmmakers create these narratives solely to be accepted in Hollywood and among mass audiences, perhaps incorporating more positive messaging incrementally may shift the landscape of negative depictions of Blacks in the media. Movies should reflect the creativity of the filmmaker, and should not be a revamped version of the same narratives that have been consistently rotated in Hollywood out of fear that audience members will not accept the storyline. More opportunities given to minority filmmakers could create a forum to create progressive images, which may begin to include counter-narratives.

Although the overall assessment of the romantic relationships in the study was not positive, it is encouraging to see Black women who did not embody traditional negative stereotypes often associated with Black women in the media. This point offered a small aspect of the positive contributions of having Black women direct their narratives. If Black filmmakers can create a counter-narrative of Black women, even when they are restricted to patriarchy-driven storylines, this proves to be a small step forward for Black female representation in Hollywood.

American culture devalues Black women, making them to work doubly hard to be loving (hooks, 2001). The transformative power of love is the foundation of social change, which has been the core of Black existence in America. There has never been a time in American society when love between Black men and women has not been threatened. Healthy self-love is imperative for Black couples' survival; it is through this self-love that we are best able to love others (hooks, 2001). Similarly, survival has been an intricate part of Black couples' lives. The bondedness essential to intimacy is compromised by a history of slavery where Black bodies were mere bartering chips (Utley, 2010). Perhaps the images in this sample reflect an attempt from women to compensate for the traumatic past endured by both Black men and women.

The notion of love is disseminated through cultural products such as films, music and other media products. Unless we want to witness more young women choosing to accept abuse as love, the political economy of the Hollywood industry must place a higher value on love. This starts with the notion of self-love. Identifying these disadvantageous consequences and advocating for self-love as an alternative provides an opportunity to move audiences beyond oppressively problematic relationships and reeducate them about the libratory erotic potential of true love (Utley, 2010).

When Black women define themselves, particularly as it relates to love, they clearly reject oppressed images. And it is this rejection that is critical Black Love depictions in films. Love's endurance is shaped by culture and Black communities' history of oppression, abuse and discrimination all contribute to how Black families and partners love one another. Perhaps the only distinct feature about Black Love is that for so long, White patriarchal ideologies combated the unification of love and matrimony within the Black community, and now Blacks demand the entitlement to the all-encompassing emotion. Media's current fixation with Black Love is not intended to distinguish itself from other cultural groups; instead, it is an outcry to opposing forces that regardless of the obstacles, institutional structures and deliberate impediment by outside forces, Black Love will always endure.

References

Brooks, D. E., & Hébert, L. P. (2006). Gender, race, and media representation. *Handbook of Gender and Communication, 16,* 297–317.

Collins, P. H. (1990). *Black feminist thought: Knowledge, consciousness, and the politics of empowerment.* New York, NY: Routledge.

Collins, P. H. (1993). Black feminist thought in the matrix of domination. In Lemert, C. *Social theory: The multicultural and classic readings* (pp. 615–625). New York, NY: Routledge.

Collins, P. H. (2004). *Black sexual politics: African Americans, gender, and the new racism.* New York, NY: Routledge.

Collins, P. H. (2016). Toward a new vision: Race, class, and gender as categories of analysis and connection. In Brewer, R. (Eds). *Race, Gender and Class* (pp. 65–75). New York, NY: Routledge.

Erigha, Maryann, "Unequal Hollywood: African Americans, women, and representation in a media industry" (2014). Dissertations available from ProQuest. AAI3634134. https://repository.upenn.edu/dissertations/AAI3634134

Erigha, M. (2018). On the margins: Black directors and the persistence of racial inequality in twenty-first century Hollywood. *Ethnic and Racial Studies, 41*(7), 1217–1234.

Gibson-Hudson, G. J. (1998). The ties that bind: Cinematic representations by black women filmmakers. *Quarterly Review of Film & Video, 15*(2), 25–44.

Guerrero, E. (1993). *Framing blackness: The African American image in film.* Philadelphia, PA: Temple University Press.

Haferkamp, C. J. (1999). Beliefs about relationships in relation to television viewing, soap opera viewing, and self-monitoring. *Current Psychology, 18*(2), 193–204.

Hendrick, C., & Hendrick, S. (1986). A theory and method of love. *Journal of Personality and Social Psychology, 50*(2), 392.

hooks, B. (2000). *All about love: New visions.* New York, NY: William Morrow.

hooks, B. (2003). The oppositional gaze: Black female spectators. In A. Jones (Ed). *The Feminism and Visual Culture Reader* (pp. 107–118). New York, NY: Routledge.

Missouri, M. A. (2015). *Black magic woman and narrative film.* New York, NY: Palgrave Macmillan.

Reynolds, T. (2002). Re-thinking a black feminist standpoint. *Ethnic and Racial Studies, 25*(4), 591–606.

Smith, J. (2013). Between colorblind and colorconscious: Contemporary Hollywood films and struggles over racial representation. *Journal of Black Studies, 44*(8), 779–797.

Staples, J. M. (2005). What's love got to do with it? Reading "Black femininity" in a media text. *Perspectives on Urban Education, 3*(2), 1–12.

Tyree, T. C. (2009). Lovin' momma and hatin' on baby mama: A comparison of misogynistic and stereotypical representations in songs about rappers' mothers and baby mamas. *Women and Language, 32*(2), 50–58.

Utley, E. A. (2010). "I Used to Love Him": Exploring the miseducation about black love and sex. *Critical Studies in Media Communication, 27*(3), 291–308.

Williams, S. R. (2015). *When and where they appear: Representations of black women in docudrama films* (Doctoral dissertation). Howard University, Washington, DC.

Index

acts of service 18, 20, 22, 24, 35, 51
agape 18, 20, 24–25
altruistic love 24–25
Asante, Amma 3, 27

baby mama 48, 57
Bamboozled 53
Bartmann, Sarah 48
Bassett, Angela 41
Beyond the Lights 3, 8, 22–25, 27,
    30, 62, 69
Belle 3, 22, 25–26
Berry, Chuck 21
Beyer, Troy 3, 30
Birth of a Nation 6
Black buck 6
Black feminist film 8–9, 59, 62, 65,
    71, 75, 77
Black feminist thought 2, 25, 58–62,
    66, 76
Black female sexuality 13, 48, 69
Black Nativity 3, 25–24, 6,
    41, 51–52
Black queen 47, 52, 54, 7
Black romances 1
Bryant, Joyce 49

Cadillac Records 3, 21, 25–26, 38,
    51–52, 62, 65
Cannon, Nick 24
Cheadle, Don 22, 38
Chism, Tina Gordan 3
The Color Purple 46
commodification 6, 49, 69
Common 22
complacent Nurturer 35, 55
controlling images 49, 59, 61–62,
    67, 69, 76
crazy black bitch 47, 51

Dandridge, Dorothy 49
Dash, Julie 9
Daughters of the Dust 9, 46
Dee, Ruby 11
diva 47
dominant culture 7–8, 48, 49, 59,
    62, 75–76
DuVernay, Ava 3, 8, 40

Ejogo, Carmen 40
Epps, Omar 21
eros 15, 20, 24–25
Eve's Bayou 3, 21, 25–28, 39, 41,
    51–52
Eurocentric 10–11, 18, 34, 55, 67

Five Love Languages 18, 20, 24
Freaknik 60
friendship love 20, 24

game-playing love 20, 24
gold digger 48
Greene, Petey 22, 38
Grier, Pam 49

Hamri, Sanaa 3
Henson, Taraji P. 22
Hooks, bell 1, 20, 25–26, 37, 73
Hottentot Venus see "Sarah Bartman"
    48–49
Hudson, Jennifer 41
hypersexualized 47–48

infidelity 20, 24–25, 37–38, 40–43,
    50, 73
intersectionality 58, 60

Jackson, Samuel L. 21, 39
James, Etta 21, 62, 65

jezebel 13, 47, 51, 60, 69
Just Wright 3, 25–26, 31

King, Coretta Scott 22, 24, 40, 51, 52
King Jr., Martin Luther 8, 22, 24
Kitt, Eartha 49
Knowles Carter, Beyonce 65

Latifah, Queen 3, 22
Lathan, Sanaa 21, 23
Lee, Spike 11, 53
Lemmons, Kasi 3, 38–39
Love & Basketball 3, 8, 21–22,
    25–26, 29, 30, 38, 42, 51, 54, 62
love conquers all 10, 20, 29–30, 32,
    37, 55, 74
love depictions 3, 10, 67, 79
Love Don't Cost a Thing 3,
    24–26, 30
Love Jones 12
ludus 17, 25

male gaze 2, 5, 13,
mammy 6, 47
mania 18, 25
Martin, Darnell 3, 38
Mbatha-Raw, Gugu 23
Medicine for Melancholy 12
Micheaux, Oscar 6
Milian, Christina 24

Parker, Nate 23
passionate love 20, 24
Peeples 3, 25–26, 32
physical Touch 18
possessive love 20, 24
practical love 20, 24
pragma 18, 25
Precious 61

Prince-Bythewood, Gina 3, 8, 9,
    22–23, 54, 63–64, 70

quality time 18, 20, 22, 23, 24, 37,
    41, 42

receiving gifts 18
romantic comedies 29, 33, 34

Selma 3, 8, 22, 24, 26, 40, 51, 52
Six Basic Love Styles 17, 20
Smollett, Jurnee 21
Something New 3, 22–23, 25–26,
    28–29, 32, 62, 65, 68
Stanton, Elizabeth C. 58
stereotypes 2–5, 7, 13, 17, 45–51,
    54, 73–74, 76, 78
storge 18, 25
superwoman 13, 47, 67

tragic mulatto 25, 47, 51, 69–70
Triangular Theory of Love 18
Townsend, Robert 46

uncle tom 6
Union, Gabrielle 38

Van Peebles, Mario 46

Waiting to Exhale 12, 46
Waters, Muddy 21, 38, 53
welfare mother 48
Whitfield, Lynn 21
White middle-class 41
White patriarchy 34, 41
words of affirmation 18,
    20–23, 29
Wright, Jeffrey 38
A Wrinkle in Time 8, 15